From Now
To Eternity

A STUDY OF
THE BOOK OF REVELATION

by

Gene M. Williams, Th.D.

Table of Contents

Chapter 1
Introduction

Revelation: Title and Significance

The translators of the King James Version of the Bible named this book *The Revelation of John*. However, it should be called *The Revelation of Jesus Christ*. The first verse of the book begins, "The Revelation of Jesus Christ...." Also, the entire book is about the Lord Jesus Christ and how He will reclaim the earth that belongs to Him.

This *Book of Revelation* is very important. C. Anderson Scott said, "Both the Bible and Christian consciousness seem to demand a Book of Revelation for their completeness and satisfaction." Also, Dr. James M. Grey wrote, "In the Book of Revelation, we return to the atmosphere of the Old Testament, at least after the third chapter, at which place the apocalyptic part begins...."

Authorship of Revelation

In the first verse of chapter 1, John writes, "The Revelation of Jesus Christ, which God gave him to show unto his servants, even the things which must shortly come to pass: and he sent and signified it by his angel unto his servant John...."

The authorship of *The Book of Revelation* is different from any other book in the Bible because it was actually given to John from the Lord Jesus Christ through an angel. It is evident that God Himself gave His Son the message to give to His servants, but He did it through the angel who gave it to His servant John. John penned what was given to him.

All of the earlier writers accepted *The Book of Revelation* as coming from the pen of John the Apostle. This was true until the middle of the third century. The exceptions to this were the Alogians, a heretical sect, which also rejected John as the author of the Gospel of John, and Caius, who was a controversialist during that period. Both rejected John as the author of *Revelation*.

However, in approximately A.D. 140, Justin Martyr wrote, "A certain man whose name was John, one of the Apostles of Christ, prophesied in the Apocalypse." Eusebius wrote that Melito, a Bishop of Sardis (A.D. 170), wrote Treatises on the Apocalypse of John. Also, Irenaeus, one of Polycarp's students wrote that John had written The Apocalypse. Tertullian, in about A.D. 200, mentions four times that *Revelation* was the work of the Apostle John. In addition, students have found, in the muratorian fragments, a quotation from *Revelation* that attributes that quotation to John the Apostle.

Many others gave credit to John, such as Clement of Alexandria and Origen, who researched the canonicity of *Revelation* and other books. Finally, Hippolytus, who was Bishop of Ostia about 240 A.D., gave credit to John the Apostle as the writer of Revelation.

The first commentary on *The Book of Revelation* was written by Bishop Victorinus. He maintains that John wrote *The Book of Revelation*. This commentary was written about 300 A.D. and is still in existence today.

Nowhere in primitive times does there seem to appear any counter-tradition but that John the Apostle was the one who wrote *The Book of Revelation*, as it was given to him by the angel sent from the Lord Jesus Christ. External evidence indicates that John wrote the book.

All internal evidence also verifies the authorship of the Apostle John. For example, the author of the book says in the first verse that his name was John. From the very beginning of Revelation to the very end, John claims to be the one who wrote the Book. Revelation 1:4 says, "John to the seven churches that are in Asia: Grace to you and peace, from him who is and who was and who is to come...." Another verse says, "I John, your brother and partaker with you in the tribulation and kingdom and patience which are in Jesus, was in the isle that is called Patmos...." (Revelation 1:9). In Revelation 22:8 John writes, "And I John am he that heard and saw these things. And when I heard and saw, I fell down to worship before the feet of the angel that showed me these things."

The higher critics have followed the inventions of a man named Dionysius, who without any reason, said that the same man could not have written *The Gospel of John* and *The Book of Revelation*. He invented one whom he called John the Presbyter of Ephesus, who was unknown to anyone before Dionysius. Still Dionysius claimed, "This Presbyter wrote the Book of Revelation." These higher critics have always tried to destroy the Bible by questioning whether or not it is authentic. They say this Presbyter wrote *Revelation* and then it was reworked, rewritten, and redone.

The author of this study rejects the higher critics because they base their conclusion on intuition, conjecture, and the idea that they are so intelligent that they can determine who wrote which books in the Bible. The man who wrote *The Gospel of John* was writing in his own style. The man who wrote *The Book of Revelation* was writing that which was given to him, and, therefore, the style is entirely different. John the Apostle wrote both books, one in his own style and the other in the style given to him.

John says in Revelation 1:2 that he bears witness of the word of God and of the testimony of Jesus Christ, even of all the things he saw. Those visions he saw, he verifies as true.

6

Promise of Blessing

In verse 3 John writes, "Blessed is he that readeth, and they that hear the words of this prophecy, and keep the things that are written therein: for the time is at hand" (Revelation 1:3). There is a blessing to those who read *Revelation*, a blessing to those who hear the prophecy, and a blessing to those who keep the things written therein. (Notice that this is a prophecy).

Many people say, "I cannot understand *The Book of Revelation*. It is so very difficult. I have heard that people go crazy because they try to interpret the book." It is true that many crazy people try to interpret the book, but *The Book of Revelation* will not drive anyone crazy. There is a real promise to those who read, study, and keep the things written in this Book.

Those who do not know the rest of the Bible find it more difficult to interpret *The Book of Revelation*. Those who understand *The Book of Revelation* are usually those who interpret on the basis of a good knowledge of the Old Testament, especially Daniel, Ezekiel, and the Olivet discourse of the Lord Jesus Christ. By comparing scripture with scripture, one can interpret Revelation fairly accurately. This does not mean any particular interpretation is perfect, but it can be very close to perfect if one uses other scriptures.

Chapter 2
The Vision of the Glorified Christ

Revelation 1:1-20

The term *Revelation* means "apocalypse," which means "the unveiling." The Greek word apo means "away from," and the Greek word kalumna means "veil." Therefore, the word *apocalypse* means "taking away the veil." The term *Revelation* is a translation of the Greek word for *apocalypse* or *apokalumna*.

Revelation reveals or unveils Jesus Christ, Who is the subject and the center of the entire book. God gave this Revelation or unveiling to His servants. John was writing so the servants could receive this message. The angel was commanded to make known to John all these apocalyptic wonders.

Recipients of the Blessing

In verses 4 and 5 John gives a greeting and also a blessing: "John to the seven churches that are in Asia: Grace to you and peace, from him who is and who was and who is to come; and from the seven Spirits that are before his throne...." (1:4-5). John is writing to the seven churches in the province of Asia Minor. Actually, these churches were only in the western part of Asia Minor and directly south of the Black Sea.

Notice he used the plural form *churches* because he was writing to more than one church. No collected body of Christians made up the church of Asia.

Source of the Blessing

John says, "Grace to you and peace, from him who is and who was and who is to come...." (1:4a). The One sending grace and peace is the Great I AM (YHWH) whom Moses met as recorded in *The Book of Exodus*. YHWH is the one that always has been, is now, and will ever be. The Holy Spirit is symbolized by the seven Spirits before His throne. Those who are interested in studying the idea of the seven spirits should read Isaiah 11:1-2.

In verse 5 John writes, "...and from Jesus Christ, who is the faithful witness, the firstborn of the dead, and the ruler of the kings of the earth. Unto him that loveth us, and loosed us from our sins by his blood" (Revelation 1:5). This greeting and blessing come from the Great I AM (YHWH), from the Holy Spirit, and then from Jesus Christ Himself. The source of all blessing is from the God Head, from the Great I AM, from the Holy Spirit, and from Jesus Christ. Jesus Christ is Prophet, Priest, and

King. In His office as Prophet, He is the faithful witness. In His office as Priest, He is the first born of the dead. As King, He is called the ruler of the kings of the earth.

Present and Future Blessing

John indicates that Jesus loves us and has loosed us from our sins. The word *loosed* is a word that is often translated "washed." Truly, He has washed us from our sins, but because of that washing, He has loosed us from our sins by His blood. The phrase could also be translated "in His blood," for both are true. "Unto him that loveth us, and loosed us from our sins by his blood" — this is true. Another translation is also true: "Unto Him that loveth us and washed us from our sins in his blood." Praise God for both truths!

Because He has loosed us from our sins and washed us in the blood, He is able to do what he mentions in verse 6: "...and he made us to be a kingdom, to be priests unto his God and Father; to him be the glory and the dominion for ever and ever. Amen" (1:6). Every believer is a priest of God. We do not need someone to go through in order to get to God, but everyone who has been born again is a priest because he has been washed in the blood. All his sins have been taken away, and he has been loosed.

In verse 7, John writes about the wonderful promise of His coming. This is His coming with clouds in majesty and glory. "He cometh" is actually what John says. No one can deny the second coming. "Behold, he cometh with the clouds...." (1:7a). Here John refers to our coming back with Him in the clouds when every eye shall see Him, not when we are raptured by Him in clouds. This will not happen at the rapture, but will happen at the Revelation when He comes and is revealed in all His power and glory, as we come back to earth with Him and He sets up His earthly kingdom. John writes, "... every eye shall see him, and they that pierced him; and all the tribes of the earth shall mourn over him. Even so, Amen" (1:7b).

In Acts 1:11, the angels indicate that when Jesus comes again, He will come in the clouds just as He left in the clouds. This will be that wonderful time of Christ's Revelation when He comes in a way that every eye will see Him. All will know whom they pierced, and every tribe of the earth will mourn. This mourning is not grief, but the idea here is that they will wail over Him. Not all of them will be ashamed or in grief because of what was done to Him, but some will wail because they know judgment is coming.

Then we see the testimony of the Almighty in verse 8 where John writes, "I am the Alpha and the Omega, saith the Lord God, who is and who was and who is to come, the Almighty." In verse 7, the statement "Even so, Amen" should go with the thought in verse 8. The statement is calculated to strengthen the faith of those who read this, and it is a virtual pledge that all these things will happen. When He says, "I am the Alpha and Omega," He is saying that all things begin in Him and all things consummate in Him. Therefore, He will see to it that all of these things will happen. He was and is and is to come; Jesus Christ is the eternal

Son of God. Here He is emphasizing His eternal nature. Also, when he says "the Almighty," he indicates that all things will be put under Him. Praise God for an Almighty, everlasting God who can perform what He promises because in Him all things begin and in Him all things will be accomplished.

Description of the Vision

Beginning with verse 9 of chapter one, the Apostle says, "I John, your brother and partaker with you in tribulation and in the kingdom and patience which are in Jesus, was in the isle that is called Patmos, for the word of God and the testimony of Jesus." Again John says he wrote this prophecy. This is the Apostle, but he does not claim his authority, or that he is any better, but he calls himself the brother of those who will be reading this and a companion with them in tribulation and in the kingdom. He has been in trials and tribulations because of the emperor who has persecuted him. That is why he is at Patmos.

The patience he is talking about is the steadfastness that comes because he has strength in the Lord Jesus Christ. Also, the word patience indicates that he is patiently waiting for the Second Coming of the Lord. He says that he was in exile because of his witness for Christ. Physically he was on Patmos, a small rocky island about twenty-four miles off the Asia Minor coast.

He says he was in the Spirit on the Lord's day. Like John, God's servants can be physically exiled, but they cannot be spiritually exiled. They cannot be cut off from God. Even though he was on Patmos, he was in the Spirit on the Lord's day. He had a wonderful experience with the Lord. The Lord's day is the first day of the week. In the early church they continued to recognize the Sabbath as the seventh day, and many of the Jewish believers would worship on that day. However, on the first day of the week they met to commemorate the resurrection of the Lord Jesus Christ and to honor the living Savior. This was called the Lord's day.

While He was in the Spirit on that day, he heard something behind him. It was the voice of the glorified Christ. John says, "I heard behind me a great voice as a trumpet" (1:10). The use of the word *as* indicates it was not actually a trumpet, but it sounded like a trumpet. It symbolized the kind of voice it was. Then the Lord gave him a commission to write the things he would see. Christ says, "What thou seest, write in a book and send it to the seven churches" (1:11). Then he mentions the seven churches: Ephesus, Smyrna, Pergamum, Thyatira, Sardis, Philadelphia, and Laodicea.

Verses 12 through 16 record John's vision of Christ in Glory: "And I turned to see the voice that spake with me. And having turned I saw seven golden candlesticks"(1:12). These were not the kind of candlesticks made of wax. The Greek word indicates that it should be translated "lamp stands." In those days, lamp stands had oil in them, and they provided light. We find out what these lamp stands represent, in verse 20 of the same chapter. Christ states that the seven candlesticks are the seven churches. Therefore, these lamp stands represent the seven churches. John says in verse 13, ". . .and in the midst of the candlesticks one like unto a son of man." So the Lord Jesus Christ was in the midst of the churches, in the midst of the lamp stands.

The idea of seven here indicates the idea of completeness. He is writing to all churches because seven is the number of perfection. Keep in mind the lamp stands are not the light; the light comes from the oil. In reality, the Holy Spirit, who is the oil, produces the light. The Lord Jesus Christ is the light of the world, but the lamp stands reflect the light.

Notice what he says next, "... one like unto a son of man, clothed with a garment down to the foot, and girt about at the breasts with a golden girdle" (1: 13). The fact that His girdle was gold indicated it was very precious. This one resembled a human being, for he was like the son of man. John saw something different about him, but he certainly resembled a human being. Notice what his dress was. He had this garment down to his feet and was girt about the breast with a golden girdle. This long robe indicated dignity and honor and the golden girdle, which was so precious, indicated righteousness. Keep in mind that the priest in the Old Testament days had a girdle, but it was not a golden girdle like this one that was given to the Lord Jesus Christ. Because He was wearing the typical garment of priests indicates that Jesus is a priest.

John continues his description of Jesus in the next verse: "And his head and his hair were white as white wool, white as snow"(1:14). In Daniel 7:9, Daniel writes about the Ancient of Days, with hair like pure wool, who was the Everlasting Father. Now we see Jesus also like the Everlasting Father, having the same kind of hair. Verse 14 indicates, "His eyes were as a flame of fire." Now this vision was like a son of man, but quite different from what a human being would look like. His eyes were as a flame of fire, indicating that He has a penetrating intelligence and the ability to read the secrets of the hearts of men.

Then John says, "...and his feet like unto burnished brass, as if it had been refined in a furnace" (1:15). His feet were like glowing white heated brass, indicating holiness. The brass also indicates judgment because every time brass is mentioned in the Old Testament it indicates judgment. The judgment of the sins of the people of the Old Testament days was laid on the brass altar. There was judgment on the animal that was burned for a substitute sacrifice that would cover the sins of the one offering the sacrifice. That was judgment. Even as the priest went from the place of sacrifice into the place of the meeting, he washed his feet and hands in a brass laver filled with water. This was necessary because his feet and hands were defiled as he walked from the place of sacrifice into the place of meeting with the Lord.

As this verse continues John writes, ". . . and his voice as the voice of many waters," (1:15b) indicating that there was a powerful voice full of majesty. The Lord of judgment Himself is the God of great power and majesty.

In verse 16, John wrote, "And he had in his right hand seven stars." We find out who the stars are in the twentieth verse. He says there, ". . .the mystery of the seven stars which thou sawest in my right hand, and the seven golden candlesticks. The seven stars are the angels of the seven churches." These seven stars represented the angels or messengers who were in His right hand, indicating that He had control of them, that He had authority over them, and that He would protect them because He had them in His right hand.

After mentioning the seven stars in verse 16 John says, ". . . out of his mouth proceeded a sharp two-edged sword." The sharp sword coming from his mouth represents the word of God. The Bible says that the word of God is like a two-edged sword. The word comes out of the mouth of God. His words are like a sharp two-edged sword. The fact that it has two edges means it has good news of grace and also news of judgment. The two edges indicate both positive and negative. When His word comes forth, there is a word of wonderful loving grace and also a word of judgment.

At the end of verse 16 John says, "...and his countenance was as the sun shineth in his strength." This did not mean that his countenance was sun; it meant that his countenance was like the sun. His shining countenance was the same thing Paul saw at his conversion, when Paul saw the tremendous light and fell and said, "Lord, what will thou have me to do?" (Acts 9:6). Now the churches are the lamp stands, the ministers are the stars, but Christ is as the sun. When He was transfigured on the Mount of Transfiguration, the brightness of his garment was as the sun. Finally, in the New Jerusalem, which we will study later, there will be no need for sun because the light will come from the Lord Jesus Himself. This light from God will be the only light we will need in that New Jerusalem, which is heaven for those who are saved.

John's Three-fold Commission

Then John receives his commission. John writes in verse 17, "And when I saw him, I fell at his feet as one dead." I would do the same thing. I would just fall at His feet as one dead. He had fear because of his adoration and respect for Christ. Verse 17 continues, "And he laid his right hand upon me, saying, Fear not." We should not fear. Why? Because He said, "I am the first and the last." He is the Creator of life, the One who sustains our life, and the One who (though we are dead) will raise us from the dead and give us life. He is the first and the last.

He continues in verse 18, "...and the Living one; and I was dead, (became dead) and behold, I am alive for evermore and I have the keys of death and of Hades." There is no need to fear because this One who is the Creator, is also the Living One who died and now is alive. Therefore, He has the keys of death and Hades. He was raised from the dead and therefore overcame death, hell, and the grave.

Hades is a prison house of the dead. Until Jesus was raised from the dead, everyone who died was there, but it was divided between those who were declared righteous and those who were not. Since the resurrection of the Lord

Jesus Christ, there is no saved person left in Hades; all who are in Hades are lost people. He was able to unlock death and Hades so that there is no fear for those of us who are saved. When He was raised from the dead, He brought, with His own resurrected body from the grave, those who were to be delivered out of Hades and now are in Paradise in the very presence of the Lord.

Now notice the key verse of the commission the risen glorified Lord Jesus Christ gives to John. One must understand this three-fold commission in order to understand the whole book. This is the outline of the book. In verse 19 He said, "Write the things which thou sawest, and the things which are, and the things which shall come to pass hereafter." John was told to write the things which he saw. These things are found in the first chapter beginning with the ninth verse. Those are the things he just finished seeing, which was the vision of the Glorified Christ.

Then he was told to write "the things which are." Those are the things that are in the day of John. Those things are in our day, for we live in the church age just like John was in the church age when he received this commission. In the second and third chapters of Revelation, he wrote "the things which are." These things were written to the seven churches, which represent all churches of all ages because of the number seven.

Also, he was told to write "the things which shall come to pass hereafter." These things begin in chapter 4, where we see the command of the Lord, "After these things I saw, and behold, a door opened in heaven, and the first voice that I heard, was as of a trumpet speaking with me, one saying, Come up hither, and I will show thee things which must come to pass hereafter" (4:1). This voice is the same as the voice John heard in chapter 1. From chapter 4 John records that which will come after the church age, after the rapture. From that point on there is no mention of church or churches until he gets through with this prophecy. At the very end of the book there is a mention of churches because there are words of exhortation that the churches should follow until the Lord Jesus Christ comes again.

A Mystery Revealed

In verse 20, Christ shows the mystery of the seven stars and the mystery of the seven golden candlesticks. The words are translated "in my right hand." The word in could be translated as "on." Therefore, it could be that the seven stars are upon His right hand or in His right hand. In any case, according to the latter part of that verse, they are the seven angels of the seven churches, and the seven candlesticks or lamp stands are the seven churches. The word angel means "messenger." Most probably, all churches have a heavenly angel that oversees the church. In addition to that, however, the word *messenger* could actually mean "the human messenger" that the Lord gives to a particular church. Keep in mind that even though a particular messenger to the church might be a heavenly angel, ultimately the word comes to the earthly human messenger (the pastor of the church) who is to give the message to the church.

Chapter 3
Message to the Church at Ephesus
Revelation 1:1-7

Before we begin studying the second and third chapters of *Revelation*, keep in mind that verse 19 of the first chapter outlines the book. Jesus said to John, "Write the things which thou hast seen and the things which are, and the things which shall come to pass hereafter" (1:19). This is the outline of the entire *Book of Revelation*. In the first chapter, he wrote the things which he had just finished seeing. Then in the second and third chapters, he wrote the things which are. Those are the things that are in the church age. John lived during the church age when he was writing, and we are living in the church age.

Then John is told to write the things that shall come to pass hereafter. When we come to Revelation 4:1, John is told he is going to see things that must be hereafter. From that point on, we do not find the word *church* at all until the sixteenth verse of the last chapter where John quotes Jesus as saying what He said His angel could testify. This is the first time the word *church* is used since chapter 3. Chapter 21, verse nine talks about the bride, which, of course, is the church; but the word *ekklesia* (church) is not used at all from the latter part of chapter 3 to Revelation 22:16.

In the second and third chapters of *Revelation*, the Lord Jesus, through John, gives messages to the angels of the churches in Asia Minor. First, these are real historical local churches that existed in Asia Minor. Second, they also symbolize many churches in any period of history. Churches like these are in existence today. There were churches like these churches all the way through history. Third, these churches are symbolic of individuals in every period of history, for there are people who resemble these churches. Fourth, these churches are very symbolic of the different periods through which the Christian churches have gone.

When I did my academic doctorate in seminary, I was supposed to know everything that I needed to know about the subject of Church History in order to be the head of a Church History department in any university. When I took my written final examination, I had to answer questions about church history for about forty hours (eight hours a day for five days).

When I began studying *The Book of Revelation* after I finished my doctorate, I was astounded that chapters 2 and 3 seemed to relate to the different phases through which the Christian churches have gone. I do not mean to say that these were not actual historical churches, but they also represent the typical church in particular periods of history. We need to deal with all four of these possibilities.

The Desirable Church

Look at the second chapter where in verse 1 John says, "To the angel of the church in Ephesus write...." The word *angel* actually means "messenger." The word *aggelos* is translated as "messenger" in the New Testament, but sometimes it is translated "angel." When it is translated "angel," most of the time it means a heavenly angel or a heavenly messenger. Undoubtedly, God has an angel that looks after individual local churches. However, He is writing to the messengers who probably came from Asia Minor to see John on the island of Patmos. He is giving the messengers to those churches, probably the pastor of those churches, these particular messages to give to the churches. The word *angel* means messenger. The letters were given to earthly pastors.

The first letter is written to the angel of the church of Ephesus. The word *Ephesus* means "desired" or "desirable," and surely this is a church that is desirable. He wrote, "These things sayeth he that holdeth the seventh stars in His right hand and He that walketh in the midst of the golden lamp stands" (2:1). He tells us who the stars are and what the lamp stands are in verse 20 of chapter 1. The stars are the messengers and the seven lamp stands are the seven churches.

Notice Jesus holds the seven stars in His right hand. This indicates He controls them. He controls the preachers, and He walks in the midst of the golden lamp stands. This means that He is in the midst of the churches. He controlled the preachers and He was in the midst of the churches in the very beginning of the church age, right after the death of the apostles, even after the death of John in the days of the apostolic fathers.

Then He says to this particular church and to churches through the ages like this, "I know thy works and thy toil and patience and how thou cannot bear evil men and didst try them that called themselves apostles, and they are not, and didst find them false" (2:2). This is a church that worked hard, and had a great deal of patience. The word patience means "steadfastness," and they were steadfast. This particular church in Asia Minor, as well as those like it, was not only one that toiled, but they would not bear evil men. In other words, they did not believe in living a carnal life. They believed in living a separated life. They tried those who said they were apostles and found them to be false. In other words, they evaluated the doctrines of those who taught and, if their teachings were not right, they rejected them. This was a church that worked hard, lived a separated life, and would not bear false teaching. They were orthodox in every manner.

This was true about that local church in Ephesus, but it is also true of many churches in existence throughout all ages, even to our day. There are orthodox churches today that work hard to win people to Jesus. These churches are not only evangelistic, but the members live separated lives. That is wonderful. That is "desirable," as the word *Ephesus* denotes. This is true of the fundamental churches of today, just as it was true of that early apostolic church.

In verse 3 He says, "And thou hast patience (steadfastness) and didst bear for my name sake and has not grown weary." This was true of the church at Ephesus and typical of the early apostolic church. Also, it is typical of some individuals in our day and throughout all the ages. It is especially typical of the fundamentalist church today. Of course, it is wonderful that people believe the word of God, work hard, and live a separated life. That is very desirable.

However, in the fourth verse He says, "But I have this against thee." The word *this* is not found in the original language. "But I have against thee" is what He actually says. He names their sin by saying, "That thou didst leave thy first love." That is very sad. Who is the first love? The first love is not evangelism. It is not baptizing many people, not doing the work of God, not just living a separated life, not just accepting doctrine and loving Bible truth. Those things are very "desirable." A person should be a separated Christian, should work hard to obey the Lord and witness for Him, and should have the right kind of belief about the Bible; but the first love is not the work of the Lord. The first love is the Lord Himself.

People can fall in love with activity, separation, and doctrine, but we should love the Lord first. If we love Jesus first, we will live a separated life, we will work hard to obey His great commission, and we will believe the truth of the word of God and reject heresy. So, even though it is desirable to live a separated life and work hard for the Lord and believe the truth, the greatest thing is to love Jesus, Who is our first love. Then all these other things will fall into place.

In verse 5 He says, "Remember therefore whence thou are fallen ...." In other words, they have fallen from loving their first love. Then he says, "And repent (which means turn back to the first love) and do the first works (that is the works you do because you love Me) or else I will come to thee and will remove thy lamp stand out of its place, except thou repent" (2:5). Now the lamp stand symbolized that they were a church. He did remove the lamp stand out of its place, for there is no longer a great church in Ephesus that witnesses for the Lord.

He writes in the sixth verse, "But this thou hast, that thou hatest the works of the Nicolaitanes." The word *Nicolaitanes* does not come from any particular doctrinal or ethnic group or any particular area of political province or anything. The word is actually made of two words put together. One is the word *Nico*, which means "to domineer." The other is *Laitanes* from which we get *laity*, meaning "people." So this word means that there were a few in the church who wanted to domineer the people. They wanted to be bosses of the people. The idea was that the clergy ought to be over the laity or that the clergy would be more prominent than the laity. Of course, this church rejected that. They hated the works of those who tried to dominate the people. The Lord Jesus said He also hates the works of those who try to dominate the people.

In verse 7 He says, "He that hath an ear, let him hear what the Spirit saith to the churches. To him that overcometh, to him will I give to eat of the tree of life, which is in the Paradise of God." Who are those who overcome? The Bible says in 1 John 5:4, "For whatsoever is begotten of God overcometh the world: and this is the victory that hath overcome the world, (even) our faith." So the way to overcome is not by trying but by trusting. Just like we are not saved by trying; we are saved by trusting. Those in that church did overcome when they trusted the Lord. Therefore, He gave these to eat of the tree of life. They will live forever and will participate in the tree of life after the resurrection.

Of course, Jesus says, "I am the way, the truth, and the life" (John 14:6). Therefore, when we trust Him, we overcome death, hell, the devil, and sin. If we trust the Lord Jesus as Savior, we will be able to eat of the tree of life and live with the Lord forever. This church at Ephesus was told that. Like this church, churches of every age are told that.

Chapter 4
Message to the Church at Smyrna
Revelation 2:8-11

The Persecuted Church

We have come through the study of the first church, and now let us look at the second church. The word *Smyrna* comes from a root word for *myrrh*. The Greek word *myrrh* means "to smash." Myrrh was a gummy substance obtained from an Arabian shrub. When the ancients made myrrh, they smashed it. It was bitter at first, but then there came a sweet fragrance. They used myrrh for medicine, for perfume, and for embalming people because it smelled so good. Remember, a woman came to put myrrh upon the Lord Jesus Christ shortly before He went to His death on the cross. Like myrrh, this particular church was smashed. The bitterness of smashing was terrible because Christians were persecuted and killed. Ultimately, however, a sweet fragrance came forth from their persecution.

Historically, Smyrna produced and traded myrrh, and in this particular city stood a temple for the worship of Tiberius. It was the seat of emperor worship. Many Jews joined in the martyrdom of one of God's preachers named Polycarp in A.D. 169. This city exists today. It was the largest city in Asia Minor and is forty miles north of Ephesus at the mouth of a small river called Meles. Even though there was great persecution in the church at Smyrna, Christianity held on better there than in any other place in Asia Minor. The church suffered much persecution; it was smashed. Many Christians in Smyrna were killed. They were burned at the stake. They were crucified (some were crucified upside down). They were split open and put on hot griddles to fry and broil and die. In the days of the early church, in the days of the martyrs, they were put in arenas and killed by lions or gladiators. People watched by the thousands in these places where they were killed.

Persecution happened in the city of Smyrna, but it also happened in the early period of the church. This is symbolic of churches of every age, for there have been churches and people that have been martyred and persecuted throughout all ages.

Christians are persecuted today in Ethiopia, China, Sudan, Turkey, Saudi Arabia, Nepal, India, Nigeria, Indonesia, and many other places. It is likely that true Christians will be persecuted in America within the next 20 years if Christ does not return before then. Yet, even though there has been persecution, the churches that were persecuted actually thrived better than the churches that were not. This is happening today in our modern era.

This church in Smyrna was very symbolic of the period the churches went through when the emperors killed so many martyrs. One book stated that the blood of the martyrs was the seed of the church. Through this period, the church grew more than it grew any other time because lost people, pagan people, and emperor worshipers saw these people willing to die for their faith as they refused to hail Caesar as lord. Instead, they boldly confessed Jesus as Lord, even though it meant death. Many were so impressed by the martyrs that they were converted to Christ. Notice in verse 8, "These things saith the first and the last, who was dead, and lived again." He is using the fact that He died and was raised from the dead to let them know that they also can be raised from the dead. The word *again* is not in the original. He was the first and the last, who died and lives.

The source of all that persecution was Satan himself, for Jesus says, "I know thy tribulation, and thy poverty, (but thou art rich), and I know the blasphemy of them which say they are Jews, and are not, but are the synagogue of Satan" (2.9). The source of all of the persecution was Satan himself. The word *synagogue* means "the coming together place," so the assembly of Satan is where all this came from. Many of the unregenerate Jews in the churches began to tell the authorities that they should kill and persecute those who were really believers. Because of the prejudice the local people had against the Jews, some of the Jews wished to twist the activity of Christians so that many Christians died. This statement is not anti-Semitic. Anyone resented by the local people might do the same thing, as seen in current persecution. He said, "I know thy tribulation, and thy poverty." They were a poor church, but they were rich because they had Christ.

He also said, "Fear not the things which thou art about to suffer: behold, the devil is about to cast some of you into prison, that you may be tried; and ye shall have tribulation ten days!" (2:10a). This happened to the church at Smyrna, but it is symbolic of the churches of all ages that are persecuted. It is very symbolic of that period the church came through after the apostolic days, after Polycarp was martyred. Then the early church went through a terrible time of tribulation. After about A.D. 170, there were ten emperors (it is significant that He says tribulation ten days) who persecuted the early church. After that, there was no more governmental persecution, so the duration of the persecution went through ten emperors and then it stopped. Then He says, "Be thou faithful unto death, and I will give thee the crown of life" (2:10b). So many of them died, but they were faithful unto death, so the Lord Jesus gave them the crown of life. They will live with Him forever.

In verse 11 He says, "He that hath an ear, let him hear what the Spirit saith unto the churches." It is the Holy Spirit speaking to John and giving the message to these pastors (angels). What does the Spirit say? He says, "He that overcometh shall not be hurt of the second death" (2:11b). It is significant that He writes this particular promise to those who are being martyred. If they are faithful they will overcome, which can only be done by faith. The second death would have no power to hurt them.

What is the second death? The second death is *gehenna*. John says in the latter part of *Revelation*, "Whosoever is not written in the book of life was cast into the lake of fire" (20:15). He also says, "All liars shall have their part in the lake which burns with fire and brimstone which is the second death" (21:8b). So the second death is everlasting separation from God in the lake of fire (*gehenna*). Those who overcome by faith are not going to be hurt by the second death, even though they will die physically.

Chapter 5
Message to the Church at Pergamum
Revelation 2:12-17

The Twice-Married Church

Now we are going to deal with the third church, the Church at Pergamum. Notice verse 12: "And to the angel of the church in Pergamum write." Pergamum was a college church. There was a great university in Pergamum, Asia Minor. This was a very intellectual church, but it was also Satan's stronghold. Immorality was rampant in the city of Pergamum. The word *Pergamus* means "twice married" or it means "elevated." So this church was elevated by being twice married. He mentions in verse 12, "These things saith He that hath a sharp two-edged sword." The word of God is like a two-edged sword. The One who has the word of God is speaking.

He says in verse 13, "I know where thou dwellest, even where Satan's throne is." A man named Attalus III, who was the priest-king of the Chaldean hierarchy, fled from Babylon from the conquering Persians and settled in Pergamus. He set up his throne there, so Satan had shifted his capital from Babylon to Pergamus. This is the message of Jesus: "And thou holdest fast my name, and didst not deny my faith, even in the days of Antipas, my witness, my faithful one, who was killed among you, where Satan dwelleth" (2:13). During this particular time, the church stood by the doctrine of the person of Jesus, and they did not deny the faith, even in those days when the witness Antipas was killed. The word *Antipas* means "instead of all." Therefore, Antipas evidently was killed instead of many others being killed.

He says, "But I have a few things against thee, because thou hast there some that hold the teaching of Balaam, who taught Balac to cast a stumbling block before the children of Israel, and to eat things sacrificed to idols, and to commit fornication" (2:14). Evidently, in the local church, there were those who were teaching compromise. That is what Balaam taught Balac to do. In order to cast a stumbling block before the children of Israel, he encouraged them to participate in idol worship, to eat things sacrificed to idols, and to commit physical fornication. The idea was they would compromise with idol worship and incorporate within the church the things related to worship in that city. There was a temple there to Zeus, the great Roman god, where there was the longest altar in the world.

Also, there were those there who held the teaching of the Nicolaitans, which (as said before) meant to domineer the laity. They believed that the clergy should

21

dominate the laity. This symbolized what happened in the period after the persecution. This is seen in the results of the first great council of the church held at Nicaea in A.D. 325. This is what happened to that individual church, but there have been churches throughout the ages that have done the same thing. They have compromised with the teachings of Babylon. Individuals have done that. Also during that particular period just after the church was persecuted, the church married the state when Constantine became emperor and put the bishop of Rome right next to him on his throne. The church compromised with the state in that the state still practiced paganism and many of the rituals of idolatry, even though Constantine said that Christianity was now the state religion of Rome.

How did this happen? Constantine was fighting with another general to see who would become the emperor of Rome. Constantine realized that about ten percent of the people in the Roman Empire were Christians. If he could have those Christians fall to his side, he would gain the balance of power. He said that he had a vision of a cross in the sky. That, he said, meant that he was to become a Christian, so he told his soldiers that if they would be baptized he would give each of them a cloak. Thousands of them were baptized. This does not mean they were saved. It just meant they gave allegiance to the religion that Constantine had indicated would be the state religion of the Roman Empire. So the state and the church were married, and the church was elevated (the idea of the word *Pergamus*) through marriage to the state. The Bishop of Rome literally sat next to the Emperor on a throne.

Because Christianity became the religion of Rome, the missionaries of the church went up into areas in northern Europe and began to compromise with the religions of the various areas. They did this just like Balaam taught Balac to do. They committed spiritual fornication. For instance, they went to Germany and found that the Germans were worshiping the god of the sun. When Winter came and the sun was far away, they used the yule log, and they put the planets on the evergreen trees. They prayed for the return of the sun. Of course, every year it returned. In order to convert there pagans to the "state religion," these missionaries instituted the ceremony of worshiping the baby Jesus, and they called it Christmas. That has to do with the word *Christ* and the word *mass*. So they instituted Christmas in the wintertime when actually there is a real probability that Jesus was born in the springtime. However, they incorporated this particular pagan ritual into Christianity. Christianity was "married" to paganism.

They also went to Gaul, which is now France, where they worshiped the goddess of fertility, called Ashteroth in the Bible. She was Easter or Aster in Gaul. She was the Babylonian goddess Istar and was often called Asherah in Canaan. She was the personification of fertility. The rabbit, which is really good in reproduction, and the egg were a part of that kind of worship. The missionaries knew that Spring was the time when Jesus died and was raised again. The worship in the Spring of the goddess Astar was called Easter. The missionaries incorporated the pagan worship of Astar into the celebration of the resurrection. Actually the word

Easter is not found in the original language. It is translated in the authorized version into the word *Easter*, though it is not found there at all in the original Greek manuscripts. The word *Easter* comes from the Babylonian goddess Astar and from the Old Testament Ashteroth. They incorporated the Easter egg and the rabbit into the time of Easter. We remember the resurrection of our Lord because that was exactly the time He was raised from the dead and taken to heaven forty days later.

In Britain, they found people who were Druids and others who practiced witchcraft and worshiped demons. In the Fall, they would use the broom in their worship. They would bring their covens together in their witchcraft and their worship of the demons. Therefore the missionaries, who went to Britain, began to incorporate that into the church. They established All Saint's Day right after Halloween, which was an incorporation of the pagan worship of demons and evil spirits and the incorporation (marriage) of witchcraft into their state religion of Rome. From the Druids and other pagans, Halloween and All Saint's Day were brought in. These are just some of the things that were incorporated. The Madonna and child with the halo around them antidated Christ by hundreds of years. Actually this was originally a picture of Nimrod and his mother, but it also developed into the Greek and Roman god Cupid and his goddess mother. Other pagan things were introduced into Christianity include the holy water; and the sign of the cross, which originated long before Christ was born; and was the sign of the tau, which is a T, used especially in Egypt in pagan worship.

In verse 16, Jesus says, "Repent therefore or else I will come to thee quickly (or suddenly), and I will I make war against them with the sword of my mouth." He will use the word of God to fight against them. Also, He mentioned in verse 12 that he had that sharp two-edged sword, which is the word of God. In verse 12, He indicated that they did not deny the faith. During that time they went through some church councils, where they hammered out some truth that was based on the word of God. These truths are the results of the council at NICEA. The statements of this council about the person of Christ exist even today. They are certainly true. They did not deny the faith, especially in relation to the person of Christ. He says in verse 17, "He that hath an ear, let him hear what the Spirit saith to the churches; To him that overcometh (overcome by faith), to him will I give the hidden manna and I will give him a white stone, (a white pebble) and in the stone a new name written, which no one knoweth but he that receiveth it." That white stone meant that those who overcame by faith had a stone indicating they were chosen to enter in into eternal life. The idea of being chosen, comes from the ancient practice of having people take pebbles from a leather sack. The one who received the black pebble was chosen for death. If a man received the white pebble, he was chosen for life.

Chapter 6
Message to the Church at Thyatira
Revelation 2:18-29

The Church of Continual Sacrifice

Revelation 2:18 begins, "And unto the angel of the church in Thyatira write...." The word *Thyatira* means "continual sacrifice." Remember the church at Ephesus represented the early apostolic church, which was in existence just after John's day. Also the Ephesian church symbolized a fundamental church today, but one that has lost its first love. After the church of the apostolic fathers, came the church at Smyrna, which represents the church of the martyrs. Churches did go through a period of persecution just as some churches are persecuted today. Then came the church at Pergamos, the church that was elevated through marriage, or married twice. This church was symbolic of the church that married the state and pagan religions.

Now we are studying the church that came after that, which is still in existence today. The church at Thyatira is the church of the continual sacrifice. Can you think of a particular church that has a sacrifice every day? The Roman Catholic Church has the sacrifice of the mass at which Jesus Christ is supposed to be sacrificed again. Every time mass is held, Jesus Christ is sacrificed. Every Sunday and all during the week, Jesus is being sacrificed in these churches. Every time they have a funeral or every time someone pays for a mass, Jesus is sacrificed. Since Roman Catholic churches exist all over the world (in every time zone), and since churches are doing this all during the day, there is probably not a moment when Jesus Christ is not supposedly being sacrificed again. Therefore, the Roman Catholic Church, like the church at Thyatira, is a church of continual sacrifice.

Apollos was the chief deity in the city of Thyatira. Emperor worship did not exist at all. The whole church is addressed from Revelation 2:18-23. Notice verse 18: "And unto the angel of the church in Thyatira write; These things saith the Son of God...." Notice when Jesus describes Himself, He always emphasizes those very things that apply to the church to which He is writing. For instance, to the church in Ephesus, He says, "this is the one that holdeth the seven stars in his right hand, who walketh in the midst of the seven golden candlesticks..." (Rev. 2:1). This applies to the Ephesus church because in the early church, Christ controlled the pastors and was in the midst of the churches. When He talks to the church at Smyrna, the church that was martyred, He says this is "the first and the last, which was dead, and is alive" (Rev. 2:8). They were going to die, and they were going to suffer persecution. Without fail, everything He says about Himself in the very beginning of each letter is applicable to the need and to the problems of that particular church.

So He says to the church at Thyatira, "these things saith the Son of God," not the son of men, not the son of Joseph, and especially not the son of Mary. This church became a fixed entity in A.D. 401. The Roman Catholic Church came into full being when, for the first time, the Bishop of Rome was the one to whom all the other bishops gave allegiance. Thus he became Pope. It was not until A.D. 401 (under Pope Innocent I) that the Catholic Church became the Roman Catholic Church. Soon came the idea of Jesus being the son of the mother Mary, and that Mary was the queen of heaven, the mother of God. They venerate Mary; they worship Mary. The fact is, one of their writings reads, "For Mary so loved the world, she gave her only begotten son that whosoever believes on him should not perish but have everlasting life." They made Mary one they worship. They say the Father won't listen to you and Jesus won't listen to you, but if you go through the mother, then she, being a woman, will listen to you and talk to Jesus for you. That is the reason they pray to Mary. When writing to the church at Thyatira, it was vital that Jesus identify Himself as the Son of God, not the son of Mary. God Almighty, embodied in the person of Jesus Christ, is worthy of worship, not Mary.

Notice He says, "And unto the angel of the church in Thyatira write; These things saith the Son of God, who hath his eyes like unto a flame of fire, and his feet are like fine brass" (Rev. 2:18). The phrase "eyes like a flame of fire" embodies the idea of omniscience. The "feet like fine brass," the feet with glowing copper, which is a hard metal, deals with judgment. Every time you see brass in the Bible, it relates to judgment. When they brought their lambs or bulls to be sacrificed, what kind of altar was it? Brass. What kind of laver did they use to symbolize the washing away of the filth that came into their lives? It was a bronze laver. Always, brass had to do with judgment. Here is the Son of God who knows everything, and as He walks, He brings judgment. This church needs to know that He brings judgment.

Commendation

Next, Christ commends the church at Thyatira: "I know thy works, and charity, and service, and faith, and thy patience, and thy works; and the last to be more than the first" (Rev. 2:19). There is no church that works harder than this church. In fact, their way of salvation is by works, through the sacraments of the church. They preach about grace. Many of their preachers preach, "You have to be saved by grace." However, their idea is that grace comes through receiving the sacraments. Especially it comes through the penance they perform in order to do away with the temporal penalty of sin. They believe in a salvation by doing, by the sacraments and by other works. They have more hospitals in this world than anybody else. They will work very hard. The monks and the nuns put bandages together and helped the poor.

Complaint

Now the Lord has a complaint, "Notwithstanding I have a few things against thee, because thou sufferest that woman Jezebel, which calleth herself a prophetess, to teach and to seduce my servants to commit fornication, and to eat things sacrificed unto idols" (Rev. 2:20). Who was Jezebel in Old Testament history? Her father was named Ethbaal, which means "one with Baal." So in one sense, symbolically she was the daughter of Baal, and Ethbaal was the high priest of the Babylonian religion, the worship of Baal and Ashteroth. She was a priestess that King Ahab married. She seduced the people of Israel to worship Baal. She tried to exterminate the prophets of God. She tried to institute Baal worship as the only religion in Israel.

What happened in Thyatira? In that particular church, there evidently was a woman that the Lord Jesus called Jezebel because she was like Jezebel of the Old Testament, in that she led the people of that church to participate in the idol worship related to Apollos, the main idol in the city of Thyatira. But in addition to that local church, this has a larger meaning. There were those in the early centuries, from the fifth century on, who led the people into paganism. They led the people into having ceremonies and rituals like the ceremonies and rituals of the Babylonian religion. Remember the church of Pergamos was the church that married the state. Because of that, they had those who held the doctrine of Baalam. They went up to spread Christianity in the North, and they allowed the people in the North to incorporate some of their old heathen worship into Christianity. During this period, heresy invaded the entire church.

The Babylonian religion is very prominent in the Roman Catholic Church. The book *The Two Babylons* by Alexander Hislop is an eye opening book about the connection between the Roman Catholic Church and the Babylonian religion. The author demonstrates that almost every tradition, almost every ceremony, almost everything found in the Roman Catholic Church is from the Babylonian religion.

So they suffered Jezebel! They suffered the religion of Jezebel to be incorporated into Christianity, and that has become the Roman Catholic religion. It is not purely Christian. Also, it has spread this all over the world. For instance, when they wanted to win the Indians of Mexico to Catholicism, the Indians worshiped the goddess of Guadeloupe. Someone said he saw a vision of our lady of Guadeloupe, who said, "I'm the goddess of Guadeloupe." They concluded, "We've been worshiping Mary all these years in the name of the goddess of Guadeloupe." As a result, all the Indians became Catholic. In Taiwan they worship the goddess of the sea and the goddess of mercy. The Roman Catholics went there and said, "We are going to set up a temple to our lady of mercy and our lady of the sea." It was very easy to get those heathen to bow down to worship a statue of Mary, our lady of mercy or our lady of the sea. They didn't change their beliefs. They still believe she is a goddess.

All over the world they have spread this very heresy. Even though intelligent Roman Catholics in the United States do not bow down to images. Yet all over the world, ignorant people are actually worshiping these statues before which they bow down. One time the author was in Chihuahua, Mexico on New Year's Eve. Jesus was supposed to be a week old. They had a little statue of baby Jesus, and all the children went up and kissed the statue. The church was very big, and it was filled with people. It was the cathedral downtown.

Condemnation

Verse 21 continues, "And I gave her space to repent of her fornication, and she repented not." There has been much time to repent. This fornication he is talking about probably was spiritual and physical fornication in the church at Thyatira, but the fornication in the Roman Catholic church is spiritual fornication. What is that? Fornication is sexual sin before or after marriage. Before the church marries Jesus, the church is the bride. If the church is unfaithful with other gods, that is spiritual fornication. Israel committed spiritual adultery because Israel was the wife of Jehovah. The church is the bride of Christ, and when any church incorporates other gods into their worship, they are committing spiritual fornication. So the church at Thyatira committed spiritual fornication in eating things sacrificed to idols. She was given time to repent of this fornication. The Roman Catholic Church, the modern-day church of continual sacrifice, has had time to repent. She has had over 1,000 years from 401 to the Reformation. Since that time she has had 500 years, but she would not repent. She has not rid herself of these heresies.

Her refusal to repent leads to severe judgment: "Behold, I will cast her into a bed, and them that commit adultery with her into great tribulation, except they repent of their deeds" (Rev. 2:22). He says here that if she doesn' t repent, he will cast her into great tribulation. Other denominations and churches are committing immorality with her in the same way. Even the kings of the world are cooperating with her in idolatry. If they fail to repent, He is going to cast them into great tribulation. The Roman Catholic Church will go into the tribulation.

The proclamation of judgment continues, "And I will kill her children with death; and all the churches shall know that I am he which searcheth the reins and hearts: and I will give unto every one of you according to your works" (Rev. 2:23). Aren't you glad you will not be judged according to your works? The church that preaches salvation by works will be judged according to its works. Those who believe that works will enable them to go to heaven quicker, rather than staying in purgatory longer, will receive according to their works. The people who are trusting in their works are going to receive according to their works. Praise the Lord, I'm going to receive according to the works of Jesus, according to what He did on the cross. I will receive according to grace because I'm trusting in the Lord. But they that trust in their works will receive according to their works.

Reward

In verse 24, He speaks to a remnant in that church, a remnant of believers: "But unto you I say, and unto the rest in Thyatira, as many as have not this doctrine, and which have not known the depths of Satan, as they speak; I will put upon you none other burden. But that which ye have already hold fast till I come" (Rev. 2:24-25). The "depths of Satan" includes all of these Satanic and Babylonian traditions and ceremonies in their religions. Since they have not embraced these things, He is not going to cast upon them any other burden. Some in this church are saved. Nevertheless, that which they have, they are to hold fast until He comes.

Just as judgment is inevitable for the unrepentant, so reward is promised for the faithful remnant. "And he that overcometh, and keepeth my works unto the end, to him will I give power over the nations" (Rev. 2:26). Isn't this significant? This church has been the one that wants to rule the nations. This church has been the political church. At times during the Holy Roman Empire, this church became the head of all the Holy Roman Empire. (I'm not talking about the early Roman Empire; I'm talking about one called the Holy Roman Empire after the fall of the empire.) Kings gave allegiance to the church. Until right before the Reformation, the church ruled the Western world. Even today, they have a great deal to do with government and have great influences in government in their attempt to rule. He says that these who are really saved, these who overcome by faith, will keep His works, not their works, but His works until the end. To those very ones, He will give authority over the nations. In other words, these will have authority over the nations in the millennial period.

These overcomers will rule with Jesus, the Supreme Authority over the nations, during the millennial period. "And he shall rule them with a rod of iron; as the vessels of a potter shall they be broken to shivers: even as I received of my Father. And I will give him the morning star. He that hath an ear, let him hear what the Spirit saith unto the churches" (Rev. 2:27-29). Who is the bright Morning Star? Jesus.

Chapter 7
Message to the Church at Sardis
Revelation 3:1-6

The Escaping Church

Now let us study the church in Sardis. Sardis was a city of the licentious worship of Cybele. The word *Sardis* means "those escaping." This church symbolizes the kind of church that escaped from Papal domination, but it also is the church that has a name that it is alive and yet is dead. A church came into existence out of the Roman Catholic Church. It was "the escaping church." That church is the Church of the Reformation, or the Protestant Church.

Chapter 3 begins, "And unto the angel of the church in Sardis write; These things saith he that hath the seven Spirits of God, and the seven stars; I know thy works, that thou hast a name that thou livest, and art dead" (Rev. 3:1). Jesus says that He has the seven Spirits. The seven Spirits refer to the seven ministrations of the Holy Spirit. He has the Holy Spirit.

He says, "I have the seven stars." At first He <u>held</u> the stars in His right hand. What are the stars? The preachers. In this church Christ does not <u>hold</u> the preachers, but he still <u>has</u> them. The Lord had the preachers in the beginning. He had Luther, He had Calvin, and He had Zwingli. Most of what they taught was true. The Westminster confession of faith is true. He had the preachers, but He didn't have the people, for the most part.

Notice what He says in the latter part of verse 1: "I know thy works, that thou hast a name that thou livest, and art dead." Evidently this local church had a name that was alive, but it was filled with dead formalism. The Reformation Church had a name that it was alive, but actually it was dead. Both the historical Protestant Church and the Protestant Church today have a name that is alive, but is actually dead. When Luther, Zwingli, Calvin, and John Knox broke away (escaped) from the Roman Church, it was partly a political thing. These preachers believed in salvation by grace and justification by faith. What they believed and what they preached were true. They went a long way, but they didn't go far enough. If they had gone one step further, it would have been a church that was alive and not dead. However, they retained one very serious error, which was infant baptism.

When Luther said, "I'll break away," many of the vassal lords of the North didn't want anything to do with the Pope. Politically, they were tired of what the

Pope was doing, how he constantly demanded money and how the Pope interfered in their affairs. The feudal or vassal lords of north Germany and Scandinavia said that they didn't want to have anything to do with the Pope. Therefore, they wrote proclamations saying that no longer were they or their subjects Roman Catholics, but from that day on they were Lutherans (followers of Luther). Of course, there were some lords who agreed with the theology of the reformers.

Did that mean they were saved — the children and all the rest of the people, such as the drunkards, adulterers, and murderers? They were all Lutheran now instead of Roman Catholic or Papists. Does that mean they were born again? Does that mean they had life? No. It meant that in a political sense they were no longer Roman Catholic but Lutheran.

Luther was encouraged by the Antibaptists to practice believers' baptism, even though not all the Antibaptists immersed. Many of the Anabaptists still sprinkled. The Anabaptists preached believers' baptism, but Luther rejected believers' baptism. Zwingli rejected believers' baptism. At first, he accepted believers' baptism, but later he came to say that infant baptism was acceptable. Luther said that children believe and that little infants believe. Calvin and Knox did the same.

In England Henry VIII said, "I want to divorce and get married again. I'm not going to listen to the Pope. I'm not going to be a Roman Catholic anymore. I'm tired of sending money out of England to the Pope. I'm weary of the Pope's control. We are going to have the Church of England, not the Church of Rome." He declared himself the head of the Church of England. Everyone became Anglican instead of Roman Catholic. Does that mean they were saved? No. They had a name that they were alive, but actually they were dead.

Even today in Protestantism the leaders are afraid their churches are going to die. Since the 1920s, they have been writing articles about how sick Protestantism is and what they are going to do to revive it. It is filled with dead formalism, the social gospel and neo-orthodoxy. In the 1930s, they began to write that they were afraid Protestantism was going to die. That's the reason they push the ecumenical movement. They want evangelicals to unite with them. They want life. They want to suck life from evangelicals, or else they are going to die. While Baptist churches and Assemblies of God, etc. are starting missions and establishing other churches, Protestant churches are saying, "We have two weak churches; let's put them together and we will have a stronger church." Even complete denominations are uniting!

One reason they do this is because they can't get enough preachers. In the church of dead formalism and liberalism, there is seldom a call from God to preach. Therefore, most of those who surrender to be preachers in dead churches are those who have the idea that they can help society by being in the ministry. I heard recently from a preacher about how the Lord led him to try to change the structure of society so that we would have a lovely community in which to live where everyone could fulfill all of his potential in the way he would like to fulfill it. This was his ministry. Their idea is that the root cause of the problem in society is poverty and not enough education." I could hardly keep from shouting out that the root cause is the sinfulness of man, the depravity of the human being. Those using the social gospel method are not getting at the root cause, but are treating the symptoms instead of the disease.

What is the Church of the Reformation? It is made up of the state churches and those churches that came out of state churches. The Lutheran church is a state church. The Reformed church (Presbyterian) is a state church. The Anglican church (which in America is the Episcopal church) is a state church. The Methodist church came out of the Anglican church. These are Protestant churches, the churches that protested against the Roman Catholic Church. A Baptist church is not a Protestant church, even though the government identifies it as such. The Nazarene church is not a Protestant church. It came out of Methodism and is thrice removed from Roman Catholicism. The Assembly of God church is not a Protestant church. Historians call these churches "sects" because they did not come from a state church. The Church of the Reformation, which includes all state churches, has a name that it is alive, but it is actually dead. Also, there are some evangelical churches (Baptist, Assembly of God, etc.) that have a name that they are alive but are dead.

Verse 2 says, "Be watchful, and strengthen the things which remain, that are ready to die: for I have not found thy works perfect before God" (Rev. 3:2). What are the things that remain? They did receive some good things from the reformers: their creed. The problem is that many Protestant ministers today reject their own creeds. The preachers don't believe the creeds. Evangelical and fundamentalist churches believe their creed. Many Reformation churches reject the virgin birth of Jesus, salvation by grace, the bodily resurrection of Jesus, and the necessity for man to be changed into a new creature. There are still some great Bible believing Protestant churches and Christians. However, most of them are very liberal.

Verse 3 issues a warning: "Remember therefore how thou hast received and heard, and hold fast, and repent. If therefore thou shalt not watch, I will come on thee as a thief, and thou shalt not know what hour I will come upon thee" (Rev. 3:3). They did receive, and they did hear. Their preachers told them the truth. This reform tradition will be here when the Lord Jesus Christ comes because there will be some who hold fast to the truth. Verse 4 continues, "Thou hast a few names even in Sardis which have not defiled their garments; and they shall walk with me in white: for they are worthy" (Rev. 3:4). As mentioned above, God does have Protestant churches that are Biblical, powerful, and alive. Also, many members of those churches are tremendous Christians.

The next two verses promise great reward for those who hold fast to the truth. "He that overcometh, the same shall be clothed in white raiment; and I will not blot out his name out of the book of life, but I will confess his name before my Father, and before his angels. He that hath an ear, let him hear what the Spirit saith unto the churches" (Rev. 3:5-6). There will be those who are saved in the Protestant churches. There are more saved in those churches than in the Roman Catholic Church. When a person is baptized when he is a baby in the Protestant Church, he is a part of the church that has a name that is alive, but actually is dead. The people in it are not saved unless later they come, through the providence of God, to trust Jesus as Savior. That doesn't mean that we should hate Roman Catholics or Protestants. We should love them.

The statement that He will not blot out a name from the book of life is a literary device that we find many times in the scripture. This doesn't mean that He blots out anybody. He is saying that even though you are part of that church which has a name that it is alive but is dead, I'm going to leave your name in the book of life. You are in a church that is dead, but I'm going to leave your name in the book of life, in spite of where you are.

If you want to find a modern church that is like a New Testament church, you should consider the following illustration. If you are looking for a lost mule that went across a river, you don't try to trace him through the river. Instead, you go to the other side of the river and pick up his tracks there. Through the Dark Ages, we can't trace the New Testament church. However, we do know that it did come through. There were New Testament churches that did come through the Dark Ages. If you want to find them, go to the other side of the Dark Ages and pick up their tracks there. They are the ones that do not follow the Catholic tradition, but the New Testament.

Please understand that the leaders of The Reformation were true men of God. They taught that the Bible is the final authority and not the traditions of men.

They preached that man is saved by grace, by the sacrifice of Christ. Many (thousands) died because they took a stand for their faith in Christ.

Also, countless laymen stood firm in the same faith. Some great dukes and princes read the Bible, were converted, and stood with the reformers.

Chapter 8
Message to the Church at Philadelphia
Revelation 3:7-13

Interpreting the Messages to the Seven Churches

The second and third chapters relate the things that are in this church age. The church age refers to both John's days and our days. Remember there are four different interpretations to each of these letters to the seven churches in Asia Minor. The first interpretation asserts that they are actual churches that existed in John's day. Another perspective states that the seven churches are representative of churches in any age. In every age there are churches like the churches at Ephesus, Laodicea, and Philadelphia. A third interpretation maintains that they are also representative of individuals throughout the ages. A particular church might have people like the Laodiceans and people like the Philadelphians. As a result, there might be a conflict going on within the church.

Finally, the seven churches are representatives of the different phases through which Christian churches have gone. For example, the first church, the church at Ephesus, represents the church after the death of the apostles. That early church is called the apostolic church. This church existed until about A.D. 150. It was very fundamental, but, in the end, lost its first love. That local church is no longer in existence. The lamp stand has been removed.

The church at Smyrna, the church of the martyr, arose right after that because of the persecution. The church at Pergamum was the church that married the state and incorporated many heathen ideas, beliefs, doctrines, and ceremonies into the church. The church at Thyatira was the church of the continual sacrifice. It is the Roman Catholic Church, which came into existence and will go into the tribulation. Then the church at Sardis was the church that escaped from Roman Catholicism and has a name that it is alive, but it is dead. That particular church is the church of the Protestant tradition, or the church of the Reformation. The leaders were evangelistic, but not missionary. However, some of God's great missionaries came from Protestantism. Many great missionaries were Anglicans.

The Evangelistic Church

Approximately 250 years after the Reformation, a church came into existence that was very strong in its missionary emphasis. The church at Philadelphia typifies this church.

33

The Church at Philadelphia was an actual church in one of the seven cities. Philadelphia had the longest duration of prosperity as a Christian city and still exists in Turkey. The name now is "City of God." Bacchus was the chief deity in John's day.

The letter to the Philadelphian church begins, "And to the angel of the church in Philadelphia write; These things saith he that is holy, he that is true, he that hath the key of David, he that openeth, and no man shutteth; and shutteth, and no man openeth" (Rev. 3:7). The way Jesus identifies Himself at the beginning of each letter is very applicable to the church to which He is writing. Remember when He said to the church at Thyatira, "Thus saith the Son of God," emphasizing that He is the Son of God, not just the son of Mary. Remember when He talked to the church at Smyrna, He said, "I'm the one that was alive and was dead, but I am alive," because they were going to be persecuted. He says certain things about Himself that should be heard by and emphasized to the particular kind of church to which He is writing.

To the church at Philadelphia He says, "These things saith he that is holy." This church was certainly a church set apart, one that was holy and true. Also He says, "he that hath the key of David, he that openeth, and no man shutteth; and shutteth, and no man openeth." The Lord is emphasizing the fact that when He closes the door, no one can open it. When He opens the door, no one can close it. This particular church was the church that practiced missionary ministry. It had an open door to evangelize the world. It arose about 150 years after the Reformation and began to flourish about 250 years after the Reformation.

An Open Door

Think about what the word *Philadelphia* means. Most people know it means "brotherly love." Philadelphia, Pennsylvania is called the city of brotherly love. Philadelphia, Pennsylvania got its name from Philadelphia in the Bible. This church had brotherly love one for another. Any church that is the kind of church it ought to be will have brotherly love. If there is anything at all that we ought to have in a church, it is brotherly love. If you have love in your heart for your brothers, it is given to you by the Lord. Not only is it true that you should love the brothers, but if you love the brothers, you are going to love the lost. You will love the lost in your community, but you will also love the lost around the world, such as those in India, Africa, Asia, and everywhere else. Jesus said, "When I shut, no man can open. When I open, no man can shut."

When I went into evangelism, friends told me that if I continued to speak the way I do, before long all the doors would be shut and that I wouldn't have any place to preach because I preach hard against sin. Also they said, "First of all, the young people are not going to come." You know what I found out? The young people came. Many times one-half the auditorium would be filled with teenagers. I didn't try to act like I was 16. I acted my age. I told it like it is in love. You don't have to be ugly when you tell it like it is. Many young preachers make that mistake. They tell it like it is, but tell it like they are mad at the congregation. You tell it like it is and you let them know you love them, and they will respond; they will hear and give heed.

God set before me an open door that nobody could close. He opened so many doors that I was booked for revivals four years in advance. God is a God of the open door. And the same thing is true with you. When God opens the door, no man can close it. When God closes the door, I don't care who a person is, he can't open it. When God opens the door for you, there is no one who can close it. Keep that in mind all of your life.

He says to the church at Philadelphia, "I know thy works: behold, I have set before thee an open door, and no man can shut it: for thou hast a little strength, and hast kept my word, and hast not denied my name" (Rev. 3:8). This particular church had power and they kept the word of God. What is the difference between keeping the <u>law</u> of God and keeping the <u>Word</u> of God? Allow me to explain by using an illustration. Suppose I said, "Take out your paper and I'll give you a test. All of you must take it." And you did. That would be keeping the <u>law</u>. But suppose I said, "I wish all of you would read a book and make a report. It would be helpful to you and helpful to me. You do not have to do it, but I wish you would." And you did it. That would be keeping the <u>word</u> because you knew I wanted you to do it. Many things in the Word of God are not definite commands, but if you love the Lord, you are going to keep His Word, just like He wants you to do, because He wants you to do it. Consider another illustration. Suppose I said to my son, "You mow the lawn." If he did it, he obeyed the law. Suppose he heard me say to my wife, "I'm sure tired. I don't want to mow the lawn. I wish someone else would do it." If he did it then, that would be keeping the word.

The church at Philadelphia kept the word, not just the law. They knew the word. You have to know the word to keep it. God said to Joshua, "This book of the law shall not depart out of thy mouth; but thou shalt meditate therein day and night, that thou mayest observe to do according to all that is written therein: for then thou shalt make thy way prosperous, and then thou shalt have good success" (Joshua 1:8). The way to keep the word is to know the word. Evidently they read the Old Testament and knew the word. Any church that is like the church in Philadelphia, as it ought to be, will be a church that knows the word of God, and therefore keeps the word of God, and will have His strength. He will set before you an open door, an open door of world evangelism.

Also, the idea of keeping His word has to do with proclaiming the inerrancy of His word. Not denying His name has to do with who Jesus really is: His deity, His humanity and character. Today there are many attacks on the Bible and the person of Christ: a Philadelphian church will believe in the inerrancy of the original manuscripts of the Bible and the deity of Christ!

Now the doors are beginning to close. We are no longer in the Philadelphian age, but there are still churches like Philadelphia. We are not in the Philadelphian age, but in the Laodicean age; however, your church can be a Philadelphian church. You ought to pray that it will be and then work so that it will be. This kind of church will love the brethren, this church will know the Word, and this church will keep the Word. This church will be one that is doctrinally sound because they know the Word and keep the Word. This kind of church will believe the Word of God is true. It will not reject the inerrancy of the Bible. However, it will not keep the Word in a spirit of hate and ugliness. It will be on the basis of loving the brethren. Hate is not brotherly love. You should take a stand on the truth. You should not compromise on separation or doctrine, but you should love the brethren. The very thing that typified this church, and should typify all churches, is that it was the church of brotherly love. Jesus said that He set before it an open door. The result of obeying the Lord will be the missionary effort to get the gospel to the lost around the world. Even though the Laodician Age is here, missionary opportunities are still there for individual Philadelphian churches.

Notice verse 9: "Behold, I will make them of the synagogue of Satan, which say they are Jews, and are not, but do lie; behold, I will make them to come and worship before thy feet, and to know that I have loved thee" (Rev. 3:9). This doesn't mean they are going to worship us; it means they are going to humble themselves before the true believers of the church at Philadelphia. What is He talking about when He refers to "the synagogue of Satan, these that say they are Jews and are not"? As you know, in Asia Minor during John's lifetime, there were different communities of Jewish people. They were so afraid that there was going to be persecution against them, and that they were going to lose their businesses, that they tried to direct and initiate persecution against the children of God who were called Christians — those who trusted the Lord Jesus Christ as Savior. Many of them had joined the early churches because they were willing to say, "We hope and we believe that He is the Messiah," but they never really trusted Him as Savior. They were of the synagogue or "the coming together" of Satan.

They said they were Jews, but what is a true Jew? A spiritual seed of Abraham is one who has been saved and has been circumcised in his heart. A completed Jew, a true Israelite, is one who is a literal child of Jacob, but also trusts the Lord Jesus Christ as Savior. These who claimed to be Jews were not like that. They were not true Jews.

Promise of Rapture

The scripture says something very significant in verse 10: "Because thou hast kept the word of my patience, I also will keep thee from the hour of temptation, which shall come upon all the world, to try them that dwell upon the earth" (Rev. 3:10). The word *temptation* here is the Greek word that often is translated "tribulation." It comes from the same root as the verb *to try* later in this verse. It means "tribulation or trial." He says I am going to keep you from that hour or period of trial that will come upon all the world to try the earth dwellers. When it says to "try them that dwell upon the earth," it is a very short term in the Greek. If you translated it as short as the Greek, it would read, "to try the earth dwellers."

Who are the earth dwellers? I'm not an earth dweller. My home is in heaven, not here. There will come a time when God will send a trial upon this earth to try the earth dwellers. What does He say to this church? "I will keep you from the hour of tribulation." What does that mean? They are going to be taken out. They are not going to go through this trial. This is one of the many verses in the Bible that indicates that the church will not go through the tribulation.

Many people think there will be a partial rapture and only the church of Philadelphia will be taken out. However, Scripture indicates that every believer will be taken out. If every believer is taken out at the rapture just before the tribulation period, then what would happen to the Philadelphian church? There will be some at the church of Thyatira taken up, but they will still have enough to have their church. There will be many of the church of Sardis taken out, but actually there will still be plenty left to have their church. In the church of Laodicea, a few who have trusted the Lord will be taken, but there will be plenty left behind in that particular church to keep on having church. When the Lord comes, there will be many taken out of the church at Philadelphia because such a large percentage of these have been saved. There won't be enough of them left to keep on having church. If there were enough of them left to keep on having church, it would not be a Philadelphian church anymore. It would cease to be that kind of church. He promises these people in this kind of church — the church typified by brotherly love and world-wide evangelism, the church that keeps His Word and loves Him — that they will not go through the tribulation period. He promises in verse 10 they will be delivered from the hour of trial that will come upon all the world to try the earth dwellers. Notice this tribulation "will come upon all the world." Some say the tribulation will be only in the Middle East. No, it "will come upon all the world."

He then says, "Behold, I come quickly: hold that fast that which thou hast, that no man take thy crown" (Rev. 3:11). This doesn't mean He is going to come soon. Jesus may come today, but He was not saying through John to this particular church, "I'm coming soon." He is saying, "I come quickly. I come suddenly. When I come it will be a quick coming." Also He says, "hold that fast that which thou hast, that no man take thy crown." Why would you have to hold fast that no one get your crown? Do you have to hold on to eternal life? No, eternal life is a gift, but a crown is a reward. A crown is given on the basis of what you do, after you are saved.

Reward for Overcomers

Verse 12 continues, "Him that overcometh will I make a pillar in the temple of my God, and he shall go no more out: and I will write upon him the name of my God, and the name of the city of my God, which is new Jerusalem, which cometh down out of heaven from my God: and I will write upon him my new name" (Rev. 3:12). How does one overcome? Who is an overcomer? The one who has faith. I John 5:4 says, "For whatsoever is born of God overcometh the world: and this is the victory that overcometh the world, even our faith." The way to overcome is to have faith.

What does it mean to be a pillar in the temple? In that day, a pillar in a temple was a granite pillar or a pillar of very strong stone that would last longer than any other portion. If you go over to Greece or Turkey about which John was writing, you will find that structures still in existence may not have a roof or much else, but the pillars are there. What is the temple of our God? We are. The Bible indicates you are the temple of the Lord in two ways. First, your individual body is a temple of the Holy Spirit. Please don't call a church auditorium a "sanctuary." It is the meeting house or the auditorium. The sanctuary is our bodies. When you think of the sanctuary as the place where you really meet God, you meet God in your heart where He lives. Every believer is called the temple. He also said, "Ye are the temple," in another scripture. So the whole church is the temple.

The church at Philadelphia will be like the pillars of a temple. Jesus is the foundation, and He said He would make this church the pillars. Jesus says, " ...and I will write upon him the name of my God, and the name of the city of my God, which is new Jerusalem, which cometh down out of heaven from my God: and I will write upon him my new name" (Rev. 3:12). The fact that His name is on that church and its members indicates that it belongs to Him. When the name of Jesus is stamped on you, it means you belong to Him. He is going to write His name and the name of the New Jerusalem on you. That means you are going to the New Jerusalem; He stamped his name and address on you. The ownership and the destination are right there.

Again, He ends the message to the church of Philadelphia by saying, "He that hath an ear, let him hear what the Spirit saith unto the churches" (Rev. 3:13). This closing echoes that of previous letters and emphasizes that every individual should listen to what He says to all the churches. Notice that the church at Philadelphia is the only one of the seven to which the Lord gives no criticism.

Even though there are Evangelical Churches like the churches in Ephesus, Smyrna, and Sardis, most Evangelical Churches are like the church at Philadelphia or the Church of the Laodiceans, which is described in the next chapter.

Chapter 9
Message to the Church of the Laodiceans
Revelation 3:14-22

The People's Church

The message to the Laodicean church begins, "And unto the angel of the church of the Laodiceans write...." (Rev. 3:14). Some translations say "the church *in* Laodicea. The King James reads the way it should be translated. Instead of "the church *in* Laodicea," it is "the church of the Laodiceans." Every other message uses the word in ("in Philadelphia," "in Sardis," etc.) However, this time the text reads "of the Laodiceans." The Greek word *en* means "in," but it is not found here.

What does that mean? It means this church belongs to the members, not to God. They own it. It belongs to them. The whole meaning of the letter to the church of the Laodiceans is that they are the ones who rule the church instead of the Lord Jesus Christ. This church was owned by, possessed by, and run by the Laodiceans. The word *Laodicea* means "people ruling" or "the authority of the people." The word *Lao* means "people." The word "laity" comes from that root. The word *dikea* means "dictatorship." In fact, *dictator* comes from the same root. It means "authority" or "rulership. Remember the Nicolaitanes were those who ruled over the people. But now the very opposite is true.

Christ is saying that this particular church is the church where the people rule. There have been churches like this throughout history. There have been individuals who were in favor of this throughout history and in all churches. Today we are living in the Laodicean age where the majority of the churches are run and ruled by the people. We are in an age where the people are in authority, even in political organizations. The first World War was supposed to have been fought to save the world *for* democracy. One day there will be a war fought to save the world *from* democracy.

A constitutional republic is the best form of government man has ever devised. However, democracy is degenerating because man is degenerate. No longer do people want to go by the Constitution. Instead, they want to reinterpret the Constitution. They want to go by what the crowd says or what the majority says. The ones who can yell the loudest and tell the biggest lies the most often, are the ones who will be in control and influence the judicial system. As this book is being written, there is a fight in the Senate of the U.S.A. over whether judges should be confirmed who will make judicial decisions on the basis of the law (constitution) or public opinion. That is the way democracy will go because by nature, man is a child of wrath. I'll vote for democracy. I don't want to be under a man like Hitler. I don't want to be under the communists. But I'll guarantee you, because of the sinful nature and the selfishness and the greed of the human being, he is going to vote for what will be best for him, not what will be best for the whole, not what will be best for the future generations, but what he will get now for himself. Christians must vote on the basis of the Bible Book, not the pocket book.

We are living in the age where the people want to rule. That is the very age we are in, even in relationship to the Roman Catholic Church. In this Laodicean age, in the church that is the most totalitarian church of all, Catholics are saying, "We don't want the Pope telling us what to do. We don't want bishops telling us what to do. We want to have a say in what we believe." For example, they want priests to be able to marry. They want to be able to divorce and still remain in the Catholic Church. The Catholics are also saying, "If there is going to be a change in what we believe, we want to have a voice in that." God's truth does not change. If a Bible teaching was true five hundred years ago, how could it be changed, just because society has changed, and people demand the change. The crux of the matter is that we are living in the Laodicean age. Be sure that your church is a Philadelphian church, not a Laodicean church.

This is what takes place when deacons (or elders) begin to rule, when the people begin to rule. When the preacher preaches and they don't like what he preaches, they say, "Now, brother, you start preaching differently or we are going to let you go." And the preacher says, "All right. I don't want to lose my job. I have a good pastorium and I have a pretty good salary, so I'll compromise." Then the people really begin to rule. They tell him what to do. They tell the next man who comes as pastor the same thing. If he doesn't go for it, they try to get rid of him. Now they don't come out and say, "This man is preaching the Bible. We don't like for him to preach all the Bible." No, they will find something else wrong. They can find something wrong with everybody. They don't get mad at him for what he does wrong. They get mad at him for what he does right. However, they find something he does wrong and blow it up and get rid of him. After all, every other preacher they ever had obeyed what they said, did what they wanted, preached the way they wanted and did all the little intricate things they felt were necessary for the ministry. In short, they ruled the church. If they fire the new pastor, the church is solidified as Laodicean.

The pastor should not be a totalitarian dictator who is above the people. No member should have to bow down to him or go to him in order to get to God, like with the Roman Catholic clergy and the Nicolaitanes. At the same time, however, the people are not to rule the church. Jesus is to rule the church.

A New Testament church is not to be a democracy. That's Bible truth. It is good for the people to know what is going on. There are times when God will lead the man of God in the pulpit to say, "This is what God wants. Let's do it." There are other times he'll say, "I want your counsel. Let's pray about it and then let's vote." You have no right to vote until you pray. Jesus is to rule. The whole problem in the Laodicean Church was that it was run by the people. The word "pastor" means shepherd. A shepherd never drives the sheep, but he never follows the sheep either. He leads and feeds the sheep. A wise pastor will always be sure his flock is with him.

What happens when a church is run by the people? It is so applicable today. He says, "And unto the angel of the church of the Laodiceans write; These things saith the Amen, the faithful and true witness, the beginning of the creation of God; I know thy works, that thou art neither cold nor hot: I would thou wert cold or hot. So then because thou art lukewarm, and neither cold nor hot, I will spew thee out of my mouth" (Rev. 3:14-16). "Spew thee out of my mouth" means "to vomit." The tense of the verb means "I am about to vomit." It doesn't mean just spit. Have you ever been sick at your stomach and you wanted to get rid of it? Drink a little lukewarm water. If you drink real cold water, it won't make you sick. If you drink real hot water, it won't make you sick. But if you drink something lukewarm, it will make you sick. He said you need to be either cold or hot.

That is exactly the kind of church we have today for the most part, a moderate church. They go to church moderately. They give moderately. They drink moderately. They sin moderately. Everything is moderate. They don't want to be cold, and they don't want to be on fire. They just want to be in the middle. A fellow may say, "He's not too bad in his theology, he's a moderate. He's not a liberal; he's a moderate. Nobody wants to be a liberal. Others don't want to be conservative, so they'll just be moderate.

The word *fan* comes from the word *fanatic*, which means "to be hot." Newspapers shortened the term to *fan* to save space. Many of you are football or baseball fans. Sports fans are fanatics — those who are "hot" and "on fire" for their team. Friend, if you're not a fanatic for Jesus, then you are either cold or lukewarm. You don't have to be a nut about a particular doctrine, but you need to be on fire for Jesus. If you are not on fire, you are a Laodicean, and you are lukewarm. He says, "You make me sick at my stomach, and I'm just about to get rid of you. I'm just about to vomit you out of my mouth."

Verse 17 continues, "Because thou sayest, I am rich, and increased with goods, and have need of nothing; and knowest not that thou art wretched, and miserable, and poor, and blind, and naked" (Rev. 3:17). The Laodicean church — the lukewarm, moderate church that doesn't offend anybody — will be quite rich. Why? Because the people run things and people will give to something they run. As long as they don't have to give much of it to missions, they can keep it for themselves. They can have lovely buildings and lovely furnishings. They can have plenty. Not only is the Laodicean church today wealthy, but the society of today is quite prosperous. People in this society don't feel that they need God. They have need of nothing because they have plenty. We're living in the Laodicean age politically, economically, and ecclesiastically. He says even though you think you are rich, you are actually wretched, miserable, poor, blind, and naked. You cannot see you are naked before me, just like Adam and Eve were after they sinned.

Jesus advises the Laodicean church, "I counsel thee to buy of me gold tried in the fire, that thou mayest be rich; and white raiment, that thou mayest be clothed, and that the shame of thy nakedness do not appear; and anoint thine eyes with eyesalve, that thou mayest see" (Rev. 3:18). When gold is refined by fire, it becomes pure because all the dross has been lifted out. They needed to be clothed in the righteousness of Jesus like those who are saved. They were naked before God. They couldn't come before His presence. They needed to be clothed with the righteousness of the Lord Jesus Christ, that righteousness that came because Jesus Christ, the Lamb of God was slain for us. He says you are blind and naked, indicating you are lost. Such a church is filled with lost people. You are poor because you don't have refined gold. You need to have your eyes opened. You need to be clothed. There are so many people in the Laodicean churches who are lost. Most churches today are Laodicean, even Evangelical Churches (like Baptist, Assembly of God, etc.) Therefore, for a church to become Philadelphian, many members must repent and be saved.

He continues, "As many as I love, I rebuke and chasten: be zealous therefore, and repent" (Rev. 3:19). He is going to reprove and chasten everyone in that particular church that He loves. If you see churches going on and on and never getting reproved or chastened, mark it down that they are not true churches of God. The same is true for individuals. "Be zealous therefore, and repent." Repent, because I'm going to chasten you if I love you.

He is calling out to the Laodicean church in verse 20, even though you can apply this to a lost person. He is really saying to individuals in the church, "Behold, I stand at the door, and knock: if any man hear my voice, and open the door, I will come in to him, and will sup with him, and he with me" (Rev. 3:20). In the very beginning of the church age, Jesus held the stars in His right hand. He was in the midst of the lamp stands: in the midst of the churches. In the church at Ephesus, Christ controlled the preachers. In the church at Sardis, He had the preachers. Now here in the very end of the church age, just before Jesus comes again, Jesus is on the outside of the church, not even in the church but on the outside knocking. He is asking, "If any individual (not all of you want me) in that church wants to have fellowship with me, open the door. I'll come in and have fellowship with him and he with Me. I'll sup with him and he with Me. I'll be in him and he'll be in Me." That's the age we are in. The longer the Lord tarries, the worse it is going to become. I use this verse to witness to individuals, but actually this verse is what He says to the church at Laodicea.

Then He says, "To him that overcometh will I grant to sit with me in my throne, even as I also overcame, and am set down with my Father in his throne. He that hath an ear, let him hear what the Spirit saith unto the churches" (Rev.

3:21-22). We're going to sit with Him in thrones, those of us who are overcomers. The way to overcome is by faith. Praise the Lord that I'm on the victory side. All these things are happening in the churches in this age. I'm not upset at all. I read the last chapter. I understand. I trust Him!

Now let us see what happens after the rapture!!!

Chapter 10
The Throne in Heaven
Revelation 4:1-11

The "things which shall be hereafter" are found in Revelation 4:1 to 22:21. In chapters 4:1 to 5:4, John sees a vision of glory! Chapter 4 begins, "After this...." After what? After Laodicea! After the letters to the churches! After the church age!

Verse 1 continues, "After this I looked, and, behold, a door was opened in heaven: and the first voice which I heard was as it were of a trumpet talking with me; which said, Come up hither, and I will show thee things which must be hereafter" (Rev. 4:1). The first two words *after this* and the last word *hereafter* are translations of the same Greek word and should be translated "after these things" in both places.

The Open Door

Now the door in heaven is open. Of course, Christ is the door of salvation. Jesus said, "I am the door: by me if any man enter in, he shall be saved, and shall go in and out, and find pasture" (John 10:9). John sees this vision of the open door and a voice like a trumpet. Remember the trumpet voice in the first chapter. The Bible says that all of sudden one day "...the Lord himself shall descend from heaven with a shout, with the voice of the archangel, and with the trump of God: and the dead in Christ shall rise first" (I Thess. 4:16). John hears this voice like a trumpet. It is the voice of the Lord Jesus Christ, who also spoke in the first chapter "with a great voice, as of a trumpet" (Rev. 1:10). His voice was like a trumpet and also like many, many waters.

The voice said to John, "Come up hither, and I will show thee things which must be hereafter" (Rev. 4:1). He begins to deal with the "things which must be hereafter." In Revelation 1:19, God commanded John to write three things. Write the things which you have seen (which he wrote in the first chapter), the things which are (which he wrote in chapters 2 and 3), and the things which shall be hereafter. Here we read that the Lord said, "Come up hither, and I will show thee things which must be hereafter" (Rev. 4:1).

At this point John begins to see the "things that will be hereafter," the things in heaven and the things on earth that will come after the church age. However, the command "come up hither" was issued to John and not to the church. John didn't go up as one that was raptured, whose body was changed. John was still in his body, but he went up in a vision and saw what was going to happen after the church is raptured. John's going up was not a symbol of the rapture of the saints, even though the rapture will come immediately before those things John writes about from this point on.

John's Vision of the Throne

John saw a vision of the throne in the verses 2 through 11. While earthly thrones are tottering, at the time when the Lord Jesus Christ comes, John sees a throne in heaven. "And immediately I was in the spirit...." (Rev. 4:2). He was not raptured or in a glorified body. He was "in the spirit" and saw the "these things that would be hereafter."

John describes his vision further: " ...and, behold, a throne was set in heaven, and one sat on the throne. And he that sat was to look upon like a jasper and a sardine stone. and there was a rainbow round about the throne, in sight like unto an emerald" (Rev. 4:2-3). The throne John saw was the throne of God, and, of course, God was the One who sat on the throne. This vision of God on His throne is a symbol of God with the saints of all the ages.

The King James Version reads, "and, behold, a throne was set in heaven." This is in the imperfect tense in the Greek, so it should be translated "a throne was being set in heaven." Jasper stone in the Bible is the word used for diamond. These diamonds indicate the glory of God and the glory of Christ. The sardine stone was a blood stone, like a ruby. It symbolizes the blood sacrifice of the Lord Jesus Christ. A rainbow like an emerald encircled the throne. The rainbow is first mentioned in the Bible as a symbol of mercy. In other words, in judgment, mercy will be remembered. Remember the covenant with Noah after the flood had come upon the earth and the whole earth was destroyed by flood. God set a rainbow in the sky and said it was a sign of the covenant that He would never again destroy the world by water. When you see a beautiful rainbow, it indicates that in judgment, mercy will be remembered. Here, the rainbow is a complete circle, never ending. In the Old Testament, the diamond symbolized Benjamin, the ruby symbolized Reuben, and the emerald symbolized Judah.

The Twenty-four Elders

John saw elders around about this throne. "And round about the throne were four and twenty seats: and upon the seats I saw four and twenty elders sitting, clothed in white raiment; and they had on their heads crowns of gold" (Rev. 4:4). Actually, the word for *seats* is the word for *thrones*. These elders are not angels because angels don't sit on thrones, nor do they ever wear crowns. Also, these four and twenty elders are going to sing a redemption song. Angels can't sing redemption songs because they have never been redeemed. The elders symbolized the redeemed of all the ages.

Around about the throne were four and twenty elders who sat on thrones, signifying kingship. They are clothed in white raiment, signifying two things: the righteousness of the saints and the priesthood of the believer. The evidence of the priesthood is that they have been washed in the blood. In chapter 7, the people in heaven had washed their robes and made them white in the blood of the Lamb (7:14). Also, chapter 19 describes the Lamb's bride and all who are part of the Lamb's bride as clothed in white raiment, white and clean: fine linen, because the white linen is symbolic of the righteousness of the saints (19:14). They are clothed in the righteousness of Christ. This whiteness indicates they are washed in the blood of the Lamb. It also indicates priesthood. As believers, we can go to God through the blood of the Lord Jesus Christ and come before Him with the righteousness of the Lord Jesus Christ because we go through the blood.

They are clothed in white raiment, and they had on their heads crowns of gold. These are victors' crowns, not diadems. They are made of gold. In John's day, if a person won a race or some athletic event, he won a crown; it was a wreath around his head made of leaves. We will have a crown of gold. The leaves perish; they pass away. The victor's gold crown of righteousness is incorruptible and will not pass away. It is laid up for all of us based on the righteousness of the Lord Jesus Christ! All of these 24 elders had them, not just some of them. Every one of them had a crown of gold. In II Timothy 4:8, Paul writes about it, "There is therefore laid up for me a crown of righteousness which he said we would receive at that day." Now "that day" means the day when the Lord Jesus Christ comes for you and for me. When He comes, we are going to receive our crowns of righteousness.

What about the 24 elders? In I Chronicles 24, David divided the priests into groups. When 24 priests were present at the tabernacle, all were symbolically there. Isn't that significant? The presence of all 24 elders at the throne indicates that all the redeemed of all ages will gather around Christ's throne. We are going to be there. We are going to be sitting with Christ on thrones. We are going to have a crown of righteousness. The 24 elders are symbolic of all of us when we get to heaven to be with Him.

Notice the power from the throne in verse 5: "And out of the throne proceeded lightnings and thunderings and voices: and there were seven lamps of fire burning before the throne, which are the seven Spirits of God" (Rev. 4:5). The seven spirits of God indicate the completeness of the Holy Spirit. The seven spirits are the seven attributes of the Holy Spirit. There is one Holy Spirit, but He is everywhere.

The Sea of Glass

Notice the sea of glass in the verse 6: "And before the throne there was a sea of glass like unto crystal" (Rev. 4:6). In Exodus 24:10, Moses, Aaron, other priests, and 70 elders saw the sea of glass. "And they saw the God of Israel: and there was under his feet, as it were, a paved work of a sapphire stone, and as it were the body of heaven in his clearness" (Ex. 24:10). In other words, they saw a vision of the LORD as if He were on the firmament of the heavens. This is identical to that.

Ezekiel 1:22 also describes the plane upon which the throne of God rested: "And the likeness of the firmament upon the heads of the living creature was as the colour of the terrible crystal, stretched forth over their heads above" (Ezek. 1:22). This is an expression of beauty, splendor, and majesty. In the temple as well as the tabernacle, there was a great laver of water, which was a sea of brass. This was there for the priest's work. The bronze altar was right before the entrance into the place of meeting, so as the priests entered into the place of meeting, they had a place to wash. This was the place where the priests would pass by after the blood sacrifice was offered. As they walked from the place of the sacrifice into the place of meeting with God, they became defiled. They had to wash their hands and their feet in order to be clean and, therefore able to enter the Holy Place.

This symbolizes the Word of God and the washing of the water by the Word. Now the water is solidified. There is no more need for cleansing after this. We are not going to be defiled by the world any more. Our old nature is gone, and we will never sin against Him again. The water in the laver was for cleansing, but now it is solidified as a sea of glass, and it will no longer be necessary for people to cleanse. Later we find the martyrs from the tribulation, standing on or in this laver, right in the midst of this sea of glass.

The Four Living Creatures

Notice the four living creatures: "And before the throne there was a sea of glass like unto crystal: and in the midst of the throne, and round about the throne, were four beasts (living creatures) full of eyes before and behind" (Rev. 4:6). These are not wild beasts, but living creatures. The Greek word is *zoon*. It doesn't mean a wild beast; it means a living creature. The background is found in Ezekiel 1:1-4 and Ezekiel 10:11-22. There Ezekiel saw a vision of one with the likeness of man. He had four faces, four wings, and four hands. He was also full of eyes. The faces that Ezekiel saw were 1) the face of man, 2) the face of a lion, 3) the face of an ox, and 4) the face of an eagle. In Ezekiel these are Cherubim (covering ones).

Cherubim and Seraphim are different. You see Seraphim (burning ones) in Isaiah 6, are saying, "Holy, Holy, Holy." Seraphim relate to judgment and holiness, but Cherubim always relate to mercy. Also consider Genesis 3. The Cherubim are there to keep mankind away from the tree of life. That's mercy — keeping man from being able to eat and live physically forever in this decaying body. Also they pointed the way to the tree of life. Cherubim have to do with mercy. The living creatures are representative of the attributes of God.

Additional background is found in the camp of Israel around the tabernacle. The tabernacle was the dwelling place of God. God dwelled everywhere, but in particular, He dwelled in the tabernacle, after the glory cloud entered. The tabernacle was surrounded by certain symbols. The camp of Judah was on the East, and their standard was the emblem of a lion, just like the first cherub. There were two tribes on either side and Judah was in the middle on that East side. Then on the West side was Ephraim. There was a tribe on each side, but they were in the middle of the three tribes. Ephraim's standard on the West was the ox. Rueben was on the South with tribes on either side and Rueben in the middle. Rueben's standard was an emblem of a man. On the North camped Dan in the middle of two other tribes, and his standard was the symbol of the eagle. Once again, we have the lion, the ox, the man, and the eagle, the same as we had in Ezekiel.

Revelation 4:7 reads, "And the first beast was like a lion, and the second beast like a calf (ox), and the third beast had a face as a man, and the fourth beast was like a flying eagle." Some scholars say that these are all the creations of God. That is not so. The living creatures are Cherubim. They symbolize the qualities of God and the qualities of the Lord Jesus Christ. Likewise, Israel was round about the tabernacle, which symbolized the qualities of God. They also indicate the work of God. The word *Cherub* means "to cover." Verse 6 refers to "living creatures," but they are identified very closely with the Cherubim found in Ezekiel. These four living creatures are full of eyes before and behind (verse 6). That symbolizes the omniscience of God. He sees everything and knows everything. They have six wings, indicating eternal activity. Notice verse 8: "And the four beasts had each of them six wings about him; and they were full of eyes within: and they rest not day and night, saying, Holy, holy, holy, Lord God Almighty, which was, and is, and is to come" (Rev. 4:8). So all together, how many wings is that? Twenty-four. And they were full of eyes within. They didn't rest day and night — eternal activity.

What about the lion? This has to do with the qualities of God and the qualities of the Lord Jesus Christ. Who is the One who shows the qualities of God in the flesh? The Lord Jesus Christ! He had these same qualities. Each of the four gospels represents Jesus Christ in the same four ways that He is represented here, around about the tabernacle, and in Ezekiel. In Matthew, He is represented as the king, the lion. All over the world the lion is called the king of the beasts. The lion indicates the King of the tribe of Judah in all His majesty. In Matthew, He is represented as the King.

What about the ox? The ox was a servant who was faithful unto death just like the oxen were slaughtered and killed and sacrificed there on the altar! Likewise, Jesus was a servant who was faithful unto death. Mark represents Jesus Christ as the suffering servant, the ox, faithful unto death. The ox also indicates the supernatural strength of the Lord, for oxen are strong, even though they are servants.

Also there was a man. Luke represents Jesus as the Son of Man. Then, of course, the eagle soars above all. What does that represent? The gospel of John represents the Lord Jesus Christ as the Son of God — the One who is above all.

Worship Before the Throne

Notice the worship of the living creatures. They worshiped the LORD just like Jesus did, "saying, Holy, holy, holy, Lord God Almighty, which was, and is, and is to come" (Rev. 4:8). The living creatures and the elders worship because of the creation. According to verse 9, "And when those beasts give glory and honour and thanks to him that sat on the throne, who liveth for ever and ever, The four and twenty elders fall down before him that sat on the throne, and worship him that liveth for ever and ever, and cast their crowns before the throne, saying, Thou art worthy, O Lord, to receive glory and honour and power: for thou hast created all things, and for thy pleasure they are and were created" (Rev. 4:9-11). Here we see the worship of the living creatures also. There is something beautiful in relationship to this. In Isaiah 6, the Seraphim do the same thing. Now here we see the worship of the heavenly beings, indicating the attributes of God worshiping Him as the Creator. The attributes of God are glorifying the Eternal One through His Son the Lord Jesus Christ.

Also, you see the worship of the elders from verses 9 through 11. They cast their crowns before Him. This gives God the glory for all victory. We have victory, but how do we have victory? Through the Lord Jesus Christ, through the power of God. These crowns are crowns of victory. We are going to receive them, and are going to cast them at the Lord's feet. Even the rewards we receive for our victory are laid before Christ because of everything His power has accomplished through us. The only proper response is the same as that of the elders, for all good and perfect gifts come from above, from the Father of lights. So the only good thing you can possibly do is not through your ability, not through your flesh, but through the power of the indwelling Holy Spirit. Through you, He does it all. Therefore, He deserves all the glory for the victory, so we will cast all the evidence of the victory at the Savior's feet. The one who has really been born again would rather give his crown to Jesus than keep it for himself because it belongs to Him anyway.

Now let us see the title deed of the earth!

Chapter 11
The Lamb is Worthy
Revelation 5:1-14

The Scroll With Seven Seals

Notice the scroll with the seven seals. "And I saw in the right hand of him that sat on the throne a book written within and on the backside, sealed with seven seals" (Rev. 5:1). The one sitting on the throne is Jehovah God Almighty. This is a scroll, not a book like we know, but a book like John knew. They did not have the kind of books we have now. They had scrolls and this scroll had seven seals. Now this scroll is the title deed of all the world. "And I saw a strong angel proclaiming with a loud voice, Who is worthy to open the book, and to loose the seals thereof? And no man in heaven, nor in earth, neither under the earth, was able to open the book, neither to look thereon" (Rev. 5:2-3). John continues, "And I wept much, because no man was found worthy to open and to read the book, neither to look thereon" (Rev. 5:4). He wanted to see what was in it. Not only that, he was mourning because there was no man who was worthy to open it.

I want to take a little space to write about this scroll. Jeremiah 36:6-15 also describes a scroll, like the one in Revelation:

> And Jeremiah said, The word of the LORD came unto me, saying, Behold, Hanameel the son of Shallum thine uncle shall come unto thee, saying, Buy thee my field that is in Anathoth: for the right of redemption is thine to buy it. So Hanameel mine uncle's son came to me in the court of the prison according to the word of the LORD, and said unto me, Buy my field, I pray thee, that is in Anathoth, which is in the country of Benjamin: for the right of inheritance is thine, and the redemption is thine; buy it for thyself. Then I knew that this was the word of the LORD. And I bought the field of Hanameel my uncle's son, that was in Anathoth, and weighed him the money, even seventeen shekels of silver. And I subscribed the evidence, and sealed it, and took witnesses, and weighed him the money in the balances. So I took the evidence of the purchase, both that which was sealed according to the law and custom, and that which was open: And I gave the evidence of the purchase unto Baruch the son of Neriah, the son of Maaseiah, in the sight of Hanameel mine uncle's son, and in the presence of the witnesses that subscribed the book (scroll) of the purchase, before all the Jews that sat in the court of the prison. And I charged Baruch before them, saying, Thus saith the LORD of hosts, the God of Israel; Take these evidences, this

evidence of the purchase, both which is sealed, and this evidence which is open; and put them in an earthen vessel, that they may continue many days. For thus saith the LORD of hosts, the God of Israel; Houses and fields and vineyards shall be possessed again in this land (Jer. 36:8-15).

What was going to happen? There was a terrible war going on. Jeremiah had been telling Judah that they were going to be taken into captivity. In order to prove he believed that one day they would be restored and return to the land again, he bought this piece of land from his cousin. He wrote on a scroll all the evidences and the witnesses and everything. Then he rolled up the scroll and sealed it, but the outside could be read. He put the scroll in an earthen vessel to keep a long time to prove this parcel of land belonged to Jeremiah (or his heirs) because he had the right as the kinsman redeemer to purchase, or redeem, the land this fellow was selling.

This helps one to understand what this scroll was in Revelation. Just like the scroll in Jeremiah was the title deed redeemed by Jeremiah, the scroll sealed with seven seals in chapter 5 of Revelation is the title deed of all the world. The One who is worthy, the Kinsman Redeemer, the One who had the right to redeem, could open the scroll.

Who is Worthy?

Who is worthy to open the scroll? Chapter 5 answers this question: "And I saw in the right hand of him that sat on the throne a book written within and on the backside, sealed with seven seals" (Rev. 5:1). "On the backside" means it is completely full. You will understand what being completely full means later. It was a rolled up book written within and on the backside, sealed with seven seals, thus perfectly sealed and perfectly complete.

Verse 2 continues, "And I saw a strong angel proclaiming with a loud voice, Who is worthy to open the book, and to loose the seals thereof?" (Rev. 5:2). This book is the title deed of the world. Who, then, is worthy to open the seals? Who is worthy to own the whole earth?

"And no man in heaven, nor in earth, neither under the earth, was able to open the book, neither to look thereon" (Rev. 5:3). They are looking for someone who is worthy to open the book in verses 1 through 3. Then in verses 4 and 5, we notice the answer.

"And I wept much, because no man was found worthy to open and to read the book, neither to look thereon" (Rev. 5:4). It couldn't be opened. They couldn't get it open because no man was worthy to open the seals and to look in.

Verse 5 identifies the only One worthy to break the seals of the book. "And one of the elders saith unto me, Weep not: behold, the Lion of the tribe of Judah, the Root of David, hath prevailed to open the book, and to loose the seven seals thereof" (Rev. 5:5). Who is the lion of the tribe of Judah? The Lord Jesus Christ! And who is the root of David? The Lord Jesus Christ! The Lord Jesus Christ has prevailed and is worthy to open the seal. He is Creator and Redeemer!

In verses 6 and 7 we see a vision of the Lord Jesus Christ: not as the lion of the tribe of Judah, but as the Lamb. "And I beheld, and, lo, in the midst of the throne and of the four beasts, and in the midst of the elders, stood a Lamb as it had been slain, having seven horns and seven eyes, which are the seven Spirits of God sent forth into all the earth" (Rev. 5:6). The seven horns mean complete power, or omnipotence. Seven eyes mean complete knowledge because He is omniscient. The seven Spirits of God represent the Holy Spirit and omnipresence. The Spirit of God going forth over all the earth indicates omnipresence. So the Lamb is all powerful, He knows everything, and He is present every place. He is God. He had been slain before and stood in the midst of the elders.

"And he came and took the book out of the right hand of him that sat upon the throne" (Rev. 5:7). He took the book out of the Father's hand. In the next few verses John describes the worship of the living creatures and the elders.

Worthy is the Lamb

"And when he had taken the book, the four beasts and four and twenty elders fell down before the Lamb, having every one of them harps, and golden vials full of odours, which are the prayers of saints" (Rev. 5:8). John describes the four living creatures, and the twenty-four elders falling down before Him. They worship Him. These vials are filled with odors, which are the prayers of the saints. So all the saints, all of the universe, and all the heavenly beings worship Him.

"And they sung a new song, saying, Thou art worthy to take the book, and to open the seals thereof: for thou wast slain, and hast redeemed us to God by thy blood out of every kindred, and tongue, and people, and nation" (Rev. 5:9). This is a new song, one that has never been sung before. "And hast made us unto our God kings and priests: and we shall reign on the earth" (Rev. 5:10). The reason He is worthy is not merely because He is God, but because He was slain. They sang that He is worthy, for He was slain. He has redeemed with His blood all kinds of people. Amazingly, we are going to be more than just saints in heaven! We are going to be priests and kings unto our God, and we will reign. He is worthy because of this redemption.

Verse 11 further portrays the worship of the Lamb. "And I beheld, and I heard the voice of many angels round about the throne and the beasts and the elders: and the number of them was ten thousand times ten thousand, and thousands of thousands" (Rev. 5:11). We don't even know how much that is. It is simply a countless number that includes the angels.

"Saying with a loud voice, Worthy is the Lamb that was slain to receive power, and riches, and wisdom, and strength, and honour, and glory, and blessing. And every creature which is in heaven, and on the earth, and under the earth, and such as are in the sea, and all that are in them, heard I saying, Blessing, and honour, and glory, and power, be unto him that sitteth upon the throne, and unto the Lamb for ever and ever. And the four beasts said, Amen. And the four and twenty elders fell down and worshiped him that liveth for ever and ever" (Rev. 5:12-14). They proclaim, "Worthy is the Lamb," and attribute glory and honor unto the One on the throne, who is God the Father, and unto the Lamb. They fall on their faces and worship Him.

Now let's see what will happen on earth after the rapture!!

Chapter 12
The Beginning of The Tribulation
Revelation 6:1-17

We see the scene in heaven in chapters 4 and 5. Even though in heaven the seals will be opened, what happens on earth? The events on earth are the result of the breaking of the seals. Chapter 6 answers these questions. The opening of the book in heaven led to massive worship of the Lamb. As the seals are broken, many woes befall the earth and its inhabitants.

The First Seal: The Counterfeit Christ

Chapter 6 begins, "And I saw when the Lamb opened one of the seals, and I heard, as it were the noise of thunder, one of the four beasts (living creatures) saying, Come and see" (Rev. 6:1). The thunder indicates judgment, majesty, and power, but especially judgment is coming now, powerful judgment because of the majesty of the Lord God.

"And I saw, and behold a white horse: and he that sat on him had a bow; and a crown was given unto him: and he went forth conquering, and to conquer" (Rev. 6:2). He opened the seal, but he didn't say to John or the reader, "Come to see." Instead He said to rider on the horse, "come," or "come to be seen." Who is the rider on the white horse? It is not Jesus, but he wants to look like Jesus. When Jesus comes in Chapter 19 of Revelation, He also comes on a white horse, but there are many things about Jesus that are not true here. Christ comes with a crown already on His head. Christ comes with a sword proceeding out of His mouth. Christ comes and conquers period. Jesus doesn't come conquering and to conquer. Christ doesn't come with a bow, and a crown is not given Him. A crown is already His. This is not Christ. This is the one that wants to be like Christ. He is the antichrist. He is not called the antichrist in Revelation; he is called "the beast." However, he is the antichrist Paul writes about in II Thessalonians and other places. This is the one who tries to take the place of Christ. You will read about him in Matthew 24:5.

A bow was given to him and no arrow. People used to laugh when this author was a young fellow. They would say, "Oh, brother, how in the world will this man conquer with a bow but no arrow? He doesn't have an arrow. How is he going to conquer?" Well, we found out after World War II that there is such a thing as cold war. In such a war, little blood is shed, but conquering comes by political pressure, by intrigue, by diplomacy, by working within an organization like the United Nations or NATO or the European Union. This man will be a diplomatic genius, a political genius. He will take over. Anyone who tries to determine his identity is foolish. We will not know his identity. The Bible says that he is not going to be revealed until after the rapture of the saints. If you are looking for him now, you will not be able to figure out who he is, because he will be revealed only after the rapture. Until the great going away, there will be no revelation of the antichrist. He'll conquer by subterfuge. He'll conquer not by a great all-out war, but because of the threat of war and the threat of a bad economy. No arrow but a bow. A crown was given unto him. He is not going to have a crown to begin with, but later he will become a world ruler. This is actually man's last effort to bring order, peace, and economic security while still rejecting Christ.

You know what people will do? They will fall for the antichrist. America will fall for him. The Western world will fall for him. If it weren't for believers, right now they would fall for him. The only thing that keeps the world from falling for him today, or one like him, is the salt of the earth that preserves right now. The only thing that keeps him from being revealed, according to II Thessalonians 2, is that we believers are here and the Holy Spirit is in us in mighty power. That is what withholds him from being revealed until the time is right.

People today are looking for three things from government. To get elected as President of the United States, one has to promise three things. First, he has to promise there will be peace. Also, he has to promise that there will be freedom from economic insecurity. Anyone who cannot seemingly produce economic security will find it hard to get elected. Last, he must promote freedom from health problems and health fears. This includes grappling with health insurance, pre-scription drugs and all the things that relate to health, such as water pollution and air pollution. That's what people want government to give. They demand not just a government to keep things in order so they can do things, but a government must produce peace, a good economy, and health. These three things will not con-tinue during the tribulation, even though the antichrist will probably promise to provide them. The world will not have freedom from war, economic security, nor freedom from health problems. Actually, government doesn't produce a good economy. God does. Also, what a government does to help a poor economy will be effective about 18 months or two years after it is put into action.

The Second Seal: Worldwide War

The antichrist comes conquering and to conquer. He conquers, but he does not finish conquering. He never finishes. It will be a bloodless conquering to begin with, but later there will be a terrible, bloody war.

Notice verses 3-4: "And when he had opened the second seal, I heard the sec-ond beast say, Come and see. And there went out another horse that was red: and power was given to him that sat thereon to take peace from the earth, and that they should kill one another: and there was given unto him a great sword" (Rev. 6:3-4). Who had opened the second seal? The Lamb, Jesus. Red is symbolic of blood. Instead of peace that the antichrist promises, there will be war. II Thessalonians 5:3 also indicates this. A sword is a symbol of war or close combat. This will be the greatest war of all times up until that time. Power was given to this one on the horse to take peace from the earth. It will be a universal war. It will be a class war according to Matthew 24:6-7. The peace that the antichrist offers will be short-lived. What about this sword that was given to him? Verse 4 ends,"...and there was given unto him a great sword." He will be given a great weapon. It might be worse than the atomic bomb, but there is going to be a great weapon given. The weapon might be chemical or biological and even worse than any weapon available today. It is going to kill many people. Instead of peace there will be war.

The Third Seal: Economic Failure and Famine

Notice what comes next from the third seal. "And when he had opened the third seal, I heard the third beast say, Come and see. And I beheld, and lo a black horse; and he that sat on him had a pair of balances in his hand. And I heard a voice in the midst of the four beasts say, A measure of wheat for a penny, and three measures of barley for a penny; and see thou hurt not the oil and the wine" (Rev. 6:5-6). This fellow has a pair of scales in his hands. A measure of wheat for a penny. You might say, "That will be cheap." However, the word translated *penny* is the word *denarius*. In John's day, that was a day's wage. So one works all day for one measure of wheat, which is enough for one meal. In other words, if you eat a good meal, it is going to be one meal for a whole day's labor. If you eat barley, which is the lowest kind, you can have three meals. However, a whole day of labor will be required just to earn enough money to eat. How about the people who can't work?

The grain is all measured out on the scales. It is going to be a time of famine, a time of inflation like this world has never known. Instead of the man being able to deliver peace, there will be war. Instead of economic security, there will be economic insecurity and famine. This is what happens after war, especially atomic or biological war. A measure of wheat will cost a day's wages. I'm not saying a man will get a penny for a day's wages. He might get $5,000 for a day's wages. But, if he gets $5,000 for a day's wages, a loaf of bread will cost $5,000. It doesn't matter how much he gets. The fact is that the whole day of labor is given and he gets enough for only one good meal. The oil and wine indicate luxury. There will be no luxury.

The Fourth Seal: Plague, Pestilence, and Death

Next, we discover what happens after the fourth seal is opened. "And when he had opened the fourth seal, I heard the voice of the fourth beast say, Come and see. And I looked, and behold a pale horse: and his name that sat on him was Death, and Hell followed with him. And power was given unto them over the fourth part of the earth, to kill with sword, and with hunger, and with death, and with the beasts of the earth" (Rev. 6:7-8). The pale horse was a green or chrome horse or kind of greenish pale. In other words, he is the color of a corpse, a dead man.

Death comes, but Hades, that place which is now the place for those who are lost, the present hell, will swallow up all of those who die. Death comes, and then right after death, most of these people go into Hades. Power was given unto them over the fourth part of the earth "to kill with sword," which is the second seal; "and with hunger," which is the third seal; "and with death" or pestilence or disease, which is the fourth seal; and "with the beasts of the earth." All efforts to preserve sanitary conditions are useless. Pestilence, disease, and plagues break out. If there is an atomic war or biological or chemical war, fall out will rain upon all the earth. There will be horrible pestilence, and death will come upon more than 1,500,000,000 people if it happened right now. One billion, 500 million people dying in this short span— this would be one fourth the number of people now (as this is written) populating the earth. All of this happens in the first two years of the tribulation: all the plagues, AIDS, small pox, anthrax, e-coli, SARS, and many other diseases will be horrible beyond our imagining. I am so glad I'm going to be gone. Now if the Lord wanted me to go through it, He would get me ready. But the Bible says I am not going to go through it. Neither will you, if you are saved.

Also notice that the beasts of the field are going to kill people. Right here in America? There are more rats being born than any other time, and they are killing people all over the Northeast and other places. This is happening not just in America but all over the world. It is going to be a horrible time. Praise God, I'm not going to be in it. Those wild animals that are now being protected, rather than unborn children, will be the very animals that will kill many during the tribulation. HIV came from chimps and monkeys. SARS came from "beasts of the fields." Bears and wolves are killing people now.

The Fifth Seal: The Righteous Martyrs

"And when he opened the fifth seal, I saw underneath the altar the souls of them that had been slain for the word of God, and for the testimony which they held" (Rev. 6:9). These are those who are martyred during the tribulation. They were slain for the word of God and for the testimony which they held. Verse 10 continues, "And they cried with a loud voice, saying, How long, O Lord, holy and true, dost thou not judge and avenge our blood on them that dwell on the earth?" (Rev. 6:10). In our day we are not to ask God for revenge. Jesus said, "Lord, forgive them." We are not to ask for revenge, but in the tribulation they do plead for revenge on the antichrist and the earth dwellers.

These martyred saints will ultimately be avenged and rewarded with robes of righteousness. "And white robes were given unto every one of them; and it was said unto them, that they should rest yet for a little season, until their fellow servants also and their brethren, that should be killed as they were, should be ful-filled" (Rev. 6:11). In other words, at the end of the tribulation, after all the rest of them are killed, God will bring revenge. God will keep His promise. The white robes are the righteousness of the saints. We find, throughout Revelation, this idea of the white robe, the purity and righteousness of the saints given to them by the Lord Jesus Christ. These are the martyred saints. Many are Jews of the 144,000, which we are going to deal with in the next chapter. They testified of the gospel of the kingdom. They are under the altar, martyred by the antichrist directly or indirectly. This vision is not of the church age, but of the tribulation. That cry was answered in Revelation 16:4, 16:7, and 20:4.

The Sixth Seal: Cosmic Chaos

When the sixth seal is opened, a great earthquake brings chaos to both the heavens and the earth.

> And I beheld when he had opened the sixth seal, and, lo, there was a great earth-quake; and the sun became black as sackcloth of hair, and the moon became as blood; And the stars of heaven fell unto the earth, even as a fig tree casteth her untimely figs, when she is shaken of a mighty wind. And the heaven departed as a scroll when it is rolled together; and every mountain and island were moved out of their places. And the kings of the earth, and the great men, and the rich men, and the chief captains, and the mighty men, and every bondman, and every free man, hid themselves in the dens and in the rocks of the mountains; And said to the mountains and rocks, Fall on us, and hide us from the face of him that sitteth on the throne, and from the wrath of the Lamb: For the great day of his wrath is come; and who shall be able to stand? (Rev. 6:12-17).

This is the wrath of the Lamb. Great physical changes will take place on the earth. These changes could be a picture of the atomic bomb or asteroids and mete-orites. But great fear is going to fall on all these people, according to verse 15.

They are going to have a great prayer meeting, but there is not going to be any repentance in this. They will cry for the rocks and mountains to fall on them so they can hide from the wrath of the Lamb. Their plea will not be one of repen-tance, but a cry to be hidden from the calamity befalling the earth. They will want to be hidden because of the things they see in verses 12 through 14: a great earth-quake, the sun blackened, and the moon turned to blood.

"And the heaven departed as a scroll when it is rolled together; and every mountain and island were moved out of their places" (v.14). This earthquake will completely change this earth. This doesn't mean there won't be any mountains or islands; it means they are going to be changed from where they are. Maps will no longer be any good. Christ is about to win back this earth from those who have stolen it, from Satan and his followers.

Now let's find out if anyone can be saved after the rapture.

Chapter 13
Saved out of The Great Tribulation
Revelation 7:1-17

In chapters 4 and 5 we saw the scene in heaven. John is still in heaven in spirit, but he is seeing things that happen upon the earth. In chapter 6, he saw some of the tribulation on earth.

Now, let us look at chapter 7. There is a parenthesis between the sixth and seventh seal, that has two portions. The first portion is a vision of the remnant of Israel, who are sealed (verses 1-8). The second portion is a vision of the saved multitude of Gentiles during the great tribulation (verses 9-17). All of these people are saved during the tribulation.

Will people be saved during the tribulation? The answer obviously is "yes." How will they be saved? They will be saved the same way anybody else has been saved. How was Abraham saved? By the blood of the Lamb. By grace through faith. How was David saved? By the blood of the Lamb. By grace through faith. The prophets were saved the same way. We could say these Old Testament saints were saved on credit. They were saved trusting in the One who would come and atone for their sin. They didn't understand everything, but they had faith. They trusted on less evidence than we have. Their faith was counted unto them for righteousness. How did they express their faith? People expressed their faith by sacrificing clean animals, looking forward to the true and final sacrifice of the Lamb of God.

During the tribulation, people will be saved the same way, by trusting in the sacrifice of Christ. There never has been anyone saved outside the blood of the Lamb. There never will be anyone saved outside the blood of the Lamb. From the very first man to the very end of the millennial period, people will be saved by trusting the Lord Jesus Christ. The Israelites have been saved that way, the only way anyone can be saved.

The 144,000 Sealed

Read what John wrote: "And after these things I saw four angels standing on the four corners of the earth, holding the four winds of the earth, that the wind should not blow on the earth, nor on the sea, nor on any tree" (Rev. 7:1). In the Greek, the word translated *corners* means "zones" from the Greek word *Zona*. The scene is one of perfect stillness. It looked as if something was going to happen. (If the wind doesn't blow, no moisture will be brought over the land from the evaporation of the oceans; that is the reason there will be no rain for three and a half years.)

Verses 2-3 continue, "And I saw another angel ascending from the east, having the seal of the living God: and he cried with a loud voice to the four angels, to whom it was given to hurt the earth and the sea, Saying, Hurt not the earth, neither the sea, nor the trees, till we have sealed the servants of our God in their foreheads" (Rev. 7:2-3). Then he says, "And I heard the number of them which were sealed: and there were sealed an hundred and forty and four thousand of all the tribes of the children of Israel" (Rev. 7:4). One hundred and forty-four thousand Israelites. Notice I do not call them Jews. The tribes of Judah and Benjamin, which formed the Southern kingdom, were the only ones that were called Jews. However, there were a few from every tribe living in Judah. They were not called Jews until they went into captivity in Babylon. The word *Jew* comes from the word *Judah*. These are not all Jews. They are Israelites.

Levi normally is not numbered. Why is Levi numbered here? Because Dan is left out. Joseph is named instead of the tribe of Ephraim, the son of Joseph. The first and the last are the two Jewish tribes, Judah and Benjamin. They were of the Southern kingdom. John writes that they were sealed: 144,000 out of the tribes of the children of Israel. *Sealed* means that they were saved. During the tribulation there will be 144,000 Israelites saved, and they will be a kingdom of priests, a missionary nation.

God said to Israel, "You are going to be a missionary nation." They made a covenant with Him. They said if you will be our God, we will be your missionary nation. We will be a kingdom of priests. We will let the world know about you. The purpose of Israel was to be a missionary nation, but they never were (Exodus 19:5b). And God says, "Now you are going to do it." In the covenant there were certain things they were supposed to do. They have never done it. Instead, they became very proud thinking, "We are God's chosen." " Instead of being a missionary nation, some became haughty and proud.

There are certain points of a covenant that are conditional. In other words, if you do this, then I'll do that. There are other parts of the covenant, where God says, "You are going to do it and I'm going to see that you do it. When I'm through with you, you will want to do it." That is the same thing with my children and me. When my son was ten years old, there were times that I would say, "You do this and I'll to that. If you don't do this, I'll do the other." If he did the right thing, then I did something for him. However, there were other times when I would say, "You're going to do it, even if I have to knock you with a 2 x 4 right between your eyes to get your attention! I don't care how long it takes me to get you to do it; you are going to do it." God said to Israel, "There are certain things if you do, I will bless you. If you don't do it, I won't bless you. But there are some things, you are going to do before I get through with you."

One of these imperatives was that they were to be a missionary nation. At least a remnant will be a missionary nation. An so in the writing of the prophets, we get the idea that the remnant (especially in Ezekiel) is a representative of all Israel, which is true Israel, the true children of Abraham, Isaac, and Jacob, but also children of God. He says, "A remnant of you will be a missionary nation." During the tribulation period, there will be 144,000 Israelites, the remnant of Israel, who will witness to others.

The Multitude of Gentiles Saved

To whom will they witness? Notice verse 9: "After this I beheld, and, lo, a great multitude, which no man could number, of all nations, and kindreds, and people, and tongues, stood before the throne, and before the Lamb, clothed with white robes, and palms in their hands; And cried with a loud voice, saying, Salvation to our God which sitteth upon the throne, and unto the Lamb. And all the angels stood round about the throne, and about the elders and the four beasts, and fell before the throne on their faces, and worshiped God, Saying, Amen: Blessing, and glory, and wisdom, and thanksgiving, and honour, and power, and might, be unto our God for ever and ever. Amen" (Rev. 7:9-12). They are around the throne. They are praising and giving glory to God.

"And one of the elders answered, saying unto me, What are these which are arrayed in white robes? and whence came they?" (Rev. 7:13). Did anybody ever ask you a question and you didn't know the answer, and you knew they knew you didn't know the answer? And they knew that you knew that they knew you didn't know the answer? That is the way it is here. He didn't know the answer and the elder didn't expect him to answer. It got his attention. It was a rhetorical question.

"And I said unto him, Sir, thou knowest. And he said to me, These are they which came out of great tribulation, and have washed their robes, and made them white in the blood of the Lamb" (Rev. 7:14). Now dear friends, these are those who are saved during the tribulation. They are of every tribe, of every kindred, of every tongue, and a multitude that no man can number. They are going to be saved during the tribulation. These are not all the people who are saved in all the ages. Some think this is a picture of heaven with all the people who are saved from all the ages, the 144,000 meaning a perfect number for all the Israelites who will be saved. This is not the case. Look at verse 14: "And I said unto him, Sir, thou knowest. And he said to me, These are they which came out of great tribulation...." I wasn't saved out of great tribulation, but they will be. And all who are saved, whether it is now or during the tribulation or whenever it is, they "washed their robes, and made them white in the blood of the Lamb." The great multitude that no man can number is the Gentiles who are saved during the tribulation. The words in the Greek language translated "great tribulation," should be translated "the tribulation, the great." This means "the tribulation, the great one." I have been through trial, but never through the tribulation, the great one. This will come after the rapture of the church.

John further describes their worship. "Therefore are they before the throne of God, and serve him day and night in his temple: and he that sitteth on the throne shall dwell among them" (Rev. 7:15). Many of these are killed during the tribulation. This is a vision of all who are saved during the tribulation. This even includes people who were saved the last day of the tribulation. Notice verse 16: "They shall hunger no more, neither thirst any more; neither shall the sun light on them, nor any heat" (Rev. 7:16). During the tribulation there will be terrible hunger and thirst and so forth. Once they are delivered from the tribulation and enter heaven, they will no longer suffer terrible hunger and thirst. Instead, God will more than compensate for their earthly suffering and will wipe the tears from their eyes.

"For the Lamb which is in the midst of the throne shall feed them, and shall lead them unto living fountains of waters: and God shall wipe away all tears from their eyes" (Rev. 7:17). This is a picture of God wiping away all the tears of those who were saved during the tribulation. These came out of the great tribulation.

During the first three and a half years of the tribulation, there will be two witnesses. (Details are given later in this book.) They will be witnesses for the Lord. Upon hearing these witnesses, many people will be saved. Some Gentiles and the 144,000 Israelites will be saved. Then at the end of three and a half years, God will allow the two witnesses to be slain. After three and a half days their bodies will be raised again, and they will ascend to the Lord, but left upon this earth will be 144,000 Israelites. They will be persecuted. All Jews will be persecuted during the last three and a half years of the tribulation, but especially these 144,000 will go through tremendous persecution. What would you do if the antichrist's Gestapo agents were after you to kill you or to put you in jail? Try to escape. Where would you escape? Where would you hide? Caves, mountains? I'd try to go to the Amazon area or to Tibet. I'd try to go to the fringes of civilization. Where are the people that have never heard the gospel? That is where they are.

Who Can Be Saved After The Rapture

Look at II Thessalonians, Chapter 2. The Christians in Thessalonica were troubled, wondering whether they would escape the tribulation. Paul's response provides great assurance for all who are saved before the tribulation. The Bible says in II Thessalonians, "Now we beseech you, brethren, by the coming of our Lord Jesus Christ, and by our gathering together unto him...." (II Thess. 2:1). Some have said that Paul was writing to them because they were upset that Jesus was coming again. They weren't upset that Jesus was coming again. Believers are not going to be upset that Jesus is coming again. On the basis of the fact that Jesus is coming again, he says, "We beg you, brothers, by the coming of our Lord Jesus Christ and by our gathering together unto him." He is actually using the fact that Jesus is coming again and that we are going to be gathered together unto Him to calm them down. He said on the basis of these two facts that Jesus is coming again and that we are going to be gathered together unto Him "...that ye be not soon shaken in mind, or be troubled, neither by spirit, nor by letter from us, that the day of Christ is at hand" (II Thess. 2:2).

What saint would be upset that Jesus was coming again? They would be concerned if they thought they were about to go through the tribulation. They were being persecuted all the time, and they thought that the tribulation was at hand. They thought they were going to go through it, or were already in it. So Paul says here, "Don't be upset. Jesus is coming again and we are going to be gathered together unto Him, so don't be upset that the day of the Lord is a hand."

"Let no man deceive you by any means: for that day shall not come, except there come a falling away first, and that man of sin be revealed, the son of perdition" (II Thess. 2:3). This verse assures the Thessalonian Christians that the rapture would precede the tribulation.

One thing about the Anglicans who controlled the translation of the King James version of the Bible is that they were honest, when they added words. They put added words in a different kind of print, and later it has been italicized in most Bibles. If you have a cheap Bible, the printer wouldn't pay the expense or take the trouble to change the type. If you have a fairly expensive Bible, you will have words that are italicized. What does it mean when words are italicized or are in different print? When I was a little boy I used to think God italicized that, and it meant that it is more important than anything else He said. I came to find out that the italicized words were not in the original text. They added words to make the translation logical.

Can translators always translate perfectly word for word? No. Many times they have to add words in a translation from any language to make sense. The word *unknown* before the word *tongue* is always italicized in the King James translation. They should have left out the word *unknown* altogether. But at least when they added it, thinking that there must be some unknown tongue they never heard, or that the people spoke in an unknown tongue instead of just languages, they put it in a different print so that it could be distinguished as a word that was added. This shows the reader that the word was added.

Let's take out all the italicized words in this passage from II Thessalonians, and translate it directly from the Greek. "Let not anyone deceive you, because unless comes the falling away first, by no means will be revealed the man of sin, the son of perdition." Notice Paul uses the definite article before the words translated "falling away." That is the way it ought to be translated.

What is this great falling away? That is the crux of the matter here. We get the word *apostasy* from it, but the word can mean "a military retreat." It doesn't necessarily mean going away doctrinally. It can mean going away doctrinally if you are talking about doctrine. One day there will be a great going away, and then the antichrist will be revealed.

To be sure, there are other evidences concerning when he will be revealed. It will be a terrible time of apostasy. That is true. Even at the time John wrote his letters, there was great apostasy. There is even worse apostasy today. Inside the church there were days when apostasy was worse than it is at this horrible time of apostasy we are in right now. Leaders didn't believe. However, there is no apostasy taught that wasn't preached in the first three centuries in relation to the person of Jesus and ideas toward the Bible. Some of those early preachers rejected many of the books of the Bible. They also said that Jesus Christ was an aberration.

There is great apostasy today. Before the rapture, the world will see more and more apostasy. What is Paul talking about? What is this great going away? The Greek word used here is *apostasia*. This word is not used in this form anywhere else in the Bible, so we must translate on the basis of the context.

Through the context, you will know it is not talking about doctrinal apostasy. It is talking about something else. In verse 4 Paul says, "Who opposeth and exalteth himself above all that is called God, or that is worshiped; so that he as God sitteth in the temple of God, showing himself that he is God" (II Thess. 2:4). He is going to do that before the flight of Israel from Jerusalem, so it couldn't be the flight. However, until there is a great going away, he can't be revealed. What is the great going away? Well, let's see what Paul is really talking about from the context in verse 5.

"Remember ye not, that when I was yet with you, I told you these things? And now ye know what withholdeth that he might be revealed in his time" (II Thess. 2:5-6). Paul never mentioned apostasy in his previous letter, but he wrote a great deal about the rapture. When he uses the definite article before the Greek word apostasia, it meant that he had explained this to them before writing his second letter to them. They knew the very thing that keeps him from being revealed. How did they know? He said you heard me talk about it, and now you know what keeps him from being revealed.

"For the mystery of iniquity doth already work...." (II Thess. 2:7). Iniquity is already working, but it is cloaked. It is behind the curtain and it is a mystery, but it is already working. "For the mystery of iniquity doth already work: only he who now letteth will let, until he be taken out of the way" (II Thess. 2:7). The word *let* is an old English word. It means "control." A little semblance of that meaning still continues when a little boy comes to his daddy and says, "Daddy, *let* me go out and play." "Let me" means Daddy has the power to keep or the power to let. He is the one who has control. In England, a person who "lets" a house has control of the house. The One who has control in verse 7 will control until He is taken out of the way. Now, there is going to be a great going away, and until the great going away the One who controls will control and keep the antichrist from being revealed. But when that One is taken away, then the antichrist will be revealed.

Who is this one that keeps the antichrist from being revealed? The Holy Spirit dwelling in believers by the millions. We are the salt of the earth. The only reason God's great wrath and judgment doesn't fall upon this world is because we are here. That preserves this earth. When the Christians are taken out at the rapture, the Holy Spirit will still work, but not in the special sense He is working through us now, through the church, through believers since the day of Pentecost. He will work just as He did in the Old Testament days, and before Pentecost. The Bible says in verse 8, "And then shall that Wicked be revealed, whom the Lord shall consume with the spirit of his mouth, and shall destroy with the brightness of his coming: Even him, whose coming is after the working of Satan with all power and signs and lying wonders (II Thess. 2:8-9). An adjective in the Greek language that doesn't modify anything, becomes a noun. So it should be, "And then that Wicked one shall be revealed." He will be revealed after the rapture, (the going away).

No Second Chance

Paul goes on to say, "And with all deceivableness of unrighteousness in them that perish; because they received not the love of the truth, that they might be saved. And for this cause God shall send them strong delusion, that they should believe a lie: That they all might be damned who believed not the truth, but had pleasure in unrighteousness" (II Thess. 2:10-12). When Jesus comes to take us away and the antichrist is revealed, people who have turned down the truth will not be able to be saved. It says it right here. "And for this cause God shall send them strong delusion, that they should believe a lie" (II Thess. 2:11). They didn't receive the truth and so they will believe a lie, "that they all might be damned who believed not the truth, but had pleasure in unrighteousness" (II Thess. 2:12). Notice the middle of verse 10, "...because they received not the love of the truth, that they might be saved" (II Thess. 2:10). God will send strong delusion to people who did not receive the Lord, did not receive the truth that they might be saved before Jesus comes. They will believe a lie.

The definite article is before the word lie in the original language. They will believe *the* lie. The antichrist is the lie, just as Jesus Christ is the truth. They will believe all the deception of the antichrist that Paul talks about in verses 8 and 9. "Even him, whose coming is after the working of Satan with all power and signs and lying wonders, And with all deceivableness...." (II Thess. 2: 9-10). If a person you are talking to about the Lord hears the gospel and turns down the gospel; if he rejects the love of the truth, and then Jesus comes, he will not be able to be saved. God will send him strong delusion so that he will believe the lie, and he will be damned because he rejected Christ. No one can be saved at anytime unless the Holy Spirit draws him.

However, people will be saved during the tribulation. That's the point. Who will they be? People who have never heard. There is no second chance. These never had the first chance, and so until they die or receive the mark of the beast, they will still have a chance because they never heard. Where will they be found? They will be in those places on the fringes of civilization, where many of the 144,000 will run and scatter because of persecution.

There will be some who have not reached an age of accountability when the rapture occurs. Children could still be saved. There will be people under the age of accountability in America who can be saved during the tribulation. Also, there are people in America who have never heard the gospel. There are Indians in Arizona who have never heard the gospel. There are people in the ghettos of New York who have never heard the gospel. They have heard something about Jesus, but still they have never heard the gospel.

In relation to whether young children will be raptured, I've searched the scripture, but there is no answer. There are three views: that the children will be left, that the children will be taken who are under the age of accountability, and that the children of believers will be taken. I have no definite answer.

Now, we'll see demons that will overrun the earth!

Chapter 14
Judgment on the Earth
Revelation 8

The Seventh Seal: A Prelude to the Trumpets

In chapter 8, the first five verses deal with the seventh seal. All these seals have to do with judgment. It looks as if this is a horrible, awesome judgment. This seventh seal indicates completion, because the number 7 has the idea of perfection. The seven seals, the seven trumpets, and the seven personages relate to the number 7, conveying the idea of completion and that "this is the end." Out of the seventh seal comes the trumpets, and out of the seventh trumpet come other sevens. It is like a great symphony which goes through one movement, then to another movement, and then another. Each movement progresses further. Therefore, we are finding out more things, about the same thing, each time we go into a different set of sevens.

Both the seven seals and the seven trumpets have to do with the tribulation. John says, "And when he had opened the seventh seal, there was silence in heaven about the space of half an hour" (Rev. 8:1). All the hosts of heaven will become silent. Nothing will be done; nothing will be said. There will be nothing but silence because of the great, awesome judgment about to fall.

He says, "And I saw the seven angels which stood before God; and to them were given seven trumpets" (Rev. 8:2). Now we are beginning with the trumpets. At the end of the seventh seal come the trumpets. Verse 3 continues, "And another angel came and stood at the altar, having a golden censer; and there was given unto him much incense, that he should offer it with the prayers of all saints upon the golden altar which was before the throne" (Rev. 8:3). Most conservative scholars believe that this angel is Jesus because of what he does. Many times in the Old Testament, Jesus is called "the Angel of the Lord." Every time we find a physical manifestation of Jehovah, that is Jesus because He is the WORD. He is the expression of God. In the beginning was the expression and the expression was with God and the expression was God. The "logos" is the expression of God. In the Old Testament, we find "the angel of JHWH," not just any angel, but *the* angel of the LORD. This was the Lord Jesus Christ even before his manifestation in the Bethlehem manger. He has always existed.

And he stood "over" or "at" the altar. John goes on to say, "having a golden censer; and there was given unto him much incense, that he should offer it with the prayers of all saints upon the golden altar which was before the throne" (Rev. 8:3). Before the door of the old tabernacle in the outer court, before one went in to the place of meeting, there was a bronze altar representing judgment. Before the throne of God is a golden altar. Gold represents purity. John saw a golden censer and a golden altar. Actually the Lord Jesus Christ is the one through whom our prayers go. This is the case here. Through the Lord, through "another angel," go our prayers and the prayers of all the saints. They go before the throne, but they go through the "golden censer" and the "golden altar." The Father answers us because our prayers go through Jesus. If our prayers didn't go through Him, we would have no chance of the Father answering us at all.

Verse 4 provides more information about the prayers of the saints. "And the smoke of the incense, which came with the prayers of the saints, ascended up before God out of the angel's hand" (Rev. 8:4). The "smoke of the incense" is the prayers through Jesus. This also includes all that Jesus has done — all of His good works, but especially what He did at the cross along with prayers. Prayers would not ascend at all if they did not ascend through Jesus — His perfect life, His sacrificial death, and His triumphant resurrection. The heathen use smoke also, thinking the smoke goes up to their ancestors' gods. In fact, the Taoists in Taiwan take a special kind of money (not government money) and burn this special money, like heavenly money. They believe the smoke that goes up is money their dead ancestors can spend. The prayers of the saints went up before God out of the angel's hand.

The next verse indicates what Jesus, the "angel," did next. "And the angel took the censer, and filled it with fire of the altar, and cast it into the earth: and there were voices, and thunderings, and lightnings, and an earthquake" (Rev. 8:5). There is going to be a horrible judgment. This is what comes out of the last seal. All seven trumpets come out of the last seal. The judgment seems to be more and more severe.

From this point John writes about the soundings of the trumpets, which goes from chapter 8:6 through chapter 11:18. There is no reason to think that what comes next is symbolic. There are symbols in *The Book of Revelation*, but always we should take everything literally unless there is a reason to take it symbolically. Everything in the Bible should be taken literally unless one of the following is true: 1) if the context indicates it should be taken symbolically, 2) if the rest of the Bible indicates it should be taken symbolically, or 3) if history or other knowledge used by the Holy Spirit causes us to accept it as symbolic. In the verses to follow there is no reason not to take literally the events that occur. There is nothing in the context, nothing in the rest of the Bible, nothing in history, and nothing in my common sense that tells me that this should not be taken literally. Therefore, all the soundings of the trumpets are to be taken literally, even though at times there is figurative language in *The Book of Revelation*.

The First Trumpet: Vegetation Destroyed

The sounding of the trumpets begins with verse 6: "And the seven angels which had the seven trumpets prepared themselves to sound. The first angel sounded, and there followed hail and fire mingled with blood. and they were cast upon the earth: and the third part of trees were burnt up, and all green grass was burnt up" (Rev. 8:6-7). The first four of these trumpets are judgment on the earth and the things upon the earth. The last three trumpets relate to judgment on men upon the earth. In other words, the first four affect natural objects, and the last three affect man's life. However, what happens to the natural objects certainly affects men. One-third of the fruit trees and other trees are gone, green grass is gone, and the cattle can't eat grass, mankind will not have much to eat. It will be a terrible time of famine. The same thing that happened in chapter 6 also happens here. In one year, there will be a complete crop failure as a far as the grass and grain are concerned. This verse refers to a literal event.

This judgment is the fulfillment of Joel 2:31-32 and Micah 7:15. "The sun shall be turned into darkness, and the moon into blood, before the great and the terrible day of the LORD comes. And it shall come to pass, that whosoever shall call on the name of the LORD shall be delivered: for in mount Zion and in Jerusalem shall be deliverance, as the Lord hath said, and in the remnant whom the LORD shall call" (Joel 2:31-32). We see in this whole section the fulfillment of this particular prophecy.

Micah 7:15 says, "According to the days of thy coming out of the land of Egypt will I show unto him marvelous things." This has to do with the last days, especially with the remnant of believers in the last days and the way God will move upon the earth. He says that some of the things that will happen at this time were things that happened in a small way in Egypt.

What happened in Egypt? Let's look at Exodus 9:22. "And the LORD said unto Moses, Stretch forth thine hand toward heaven, that there may be hail in all the land of Egypt, upon man, and upon beast, and upon every herb of the field, throughout the land of Egypt. And Moses stretched forth his rod toward heaven: and the LORD sent thunder and hail, and the fire ran along upon the ground; and the LORD rained hail upon the land of Egypt. So there was hail, and fire mingled with the hail, very grievous, such as there was none like it in all the land of Egypt since it became a nation. And the hail smote throughout all the land of Egypt all that was in the field, both man and beast; and the hail smote every herb of the field, and brake every tree of the field. Only in the land Goshen, where the children of Israel were, was there no hail" (Exodus 9:22-26). This same thing will happen during the tribulation, and it will be a terrible time. It will be literal like it was in Egypt during Moses' day. God will do this as a form of judgment. He talks about hail and fire as it happened in Egypt, hail and fire mingled with blood. This was cast upon the earth and a third part of the trees was burned up, and all green grass was burned up.

The Second Trumpet: The Seas Become Blood

Look at the second trumpet, the burning meteorite, or asteroid, or atomic bomb. Notice what it says: "And the second angel sounded, and as it were a great mountain burning with fire was cast into the sea: and the third part of the sea became blood; And the third part of the creatures which were in the sea, and had life, died; and the third part of the ships were destroyed" (Rev. 8:8-9). When he says "as it were," he is not referring to an actual mountain, but it was like a mountain. Perhaps this great mountain is a literal meteorite. Scientists have told us that we should expect a large asteroid or meteorite to hit the earth. At this time, a third of all the fish and the creatures of the sea will be destroyed. In the Bible when we find one-third, that means less than half. It could be exactly one-third, but many times in apocalyptic literature, it just means less than half. Therefore, it could be as much as 49.99 percent. But around a third of the fish and the creatures of the sea will be destroyed including whales, oysters, fish, shrimp, and clams. It will cause disease and terrible pestilence.

The Third Trumpet: Water Becomes Wormwood

Verse 10 records the sounding of the third trumpet. "And the third angel sounded, and there fell a great star from heaven...." (Rev. 8:10). The Bible says God knows the names of all the stars. One may say, "There are too many stars!" He knows you and He knows your name. He knows everyone else because He is God. I hurt when people think God is such a little God that He couldn't do this. He knows the name of all the stars. This is perhaps a comet or some other kind of star. Scientists say it is clear that eventually a comet will hit the earth, or at least the gas (called the tail) of a comet will touch the earth.

The great star falling from heaven will create another calamity. "And the third angel sounded, and there fell a great star from heaven, burning as it were a lamp, and it fell upon the third part of the rivers, and upon the fountains of waters; And the name of the star is called Wormwood: and the third part of the waters became wormwood; and many men died of the waters, because they were made bitter (Rev. 8:10-11). The word for *wormwood* (Greek: "apsinthos") refers to a bitter, intoxicating, poisonous herb. It produces convulsions and it paralyzes the person, leading to death. The waters will act the same way that wormwood does!

Jeremiah 9:13-15 also mentions wormwood. "And the LORD saith, Because they have forsaken my law which I set before them, and have not obeyed my voice, neither walked therein; But have walked after the imagination of their own heart, and after Baalim, which their fathers taught them: Therefore thus saith the LORD of hosts, the God of Israel; Behold, I will feed them, even this people, with wormwood, and give them water of gall to drink" (Jer. 9:13-15). This is a prophecy of what will happen during the time of the tribulation. People are going to be given this kind of water to drink. I don't know what it is going to be. It might be toxins that are poured into the waters. It will be a miraculous thing. God is going to allow a third of all the streams and artesian wells to become completely polluted. These waters will be polluted with a terrible kind of substance that will have the same results as when people take wormwood. The bitter, poisonous water will lead to convulsions, paralysis, and then death.

The Fourth Trumpet: The Earth is Darkened

When the fourth angel sounds, conditions on earth get even worse. "And the fourth angel sounded, and the third part of the sun was smitten, and the third part of the moon, and the third part of the stars; so as the third part of them was darkened, and the day shone not for a third part of it, and the night likewise" (Rev. 8:12). One-third of all the light and heat that this earth receives will be taken away by the Lord. Remember Micah the prophet said the things that are going to happen in this day will be like the things that happened in Egypt. This happened in Egypt when darkness came on Egypt, and they couldn't see. This is going to be a terrible time because this disaster will disturb the seasons. Therefore, it will disturb the ripening of the fruit and the harvest.

Could it be that all this water pollution will be caused by man? Could it be that the sun, moon and star will not be seen because of pollution in the air? In any case, it will happen.

Isaiah warns of impending judgment by referring to the "day of the LORD." "Behold, the day of the LORD cometh, cruel both with wrath and fierce anger, to lay the land desolate: and he shall destroy the sinners thereof out of it. For the stars of heaven and the constellations thereof shall not give their light: the sun shall be darkened in his going forth, and the moon shall not cause her light to shine. And I will punish the world for their evil, and the wicked for their iniquity; and I will cause the arrogancy of the proud to cease, and will lay low the haughtiness of the terrible" (Isaiah 13:9-11). When he said the "day of the Lord," he was talking about this time that we are reading about in Revelation.

In verse 13, John talks about something else that happens right after the earth is darkened. "And I beheld, and heard an angel flying through the midst of heaven, saying with a loud voice, Woe, woe, woe, to the inhabiters of the earth by reason of the other voices of the trumpet of the three angels, which are yet to sound!" (Rev. 8:13). He is warning those who live on the earth, "You had better get right. You had better repent." They will not repent, of course. All of the way through, offers of mercy seem to be given, but the earth dwellers never respond. He is saying; "Woe, woe, woe," three woes.

Chapter 15
Judgment on the Earth Dwellers
Revelation 9

The last three trumpets begin sounding in the ninth chapter. The resulting woes go beyond the physical world. Other agencies are called in, and evil spirits are permitted to overrun the world.

The Fifth Trumpet: Demonic Tormentors Unleashed

Chapter 9 begins, "And the fifth angel sounded, and I saw a star fall from heaven unto the earth: and to him was given the key of the bottomless pit" (Rev. 9:1). This star is called a "him." Who could this be? Jesus is called "a bright and morning star." And what about the stars Christ held in His right hand, which are angels of the churches? Here we find a fallen star. This fallen star is either Lucifer, or it is the angel of Revelation 20 that binds Lucifer. I don't know exactly which one this star represents. The angel, who came down from heaven in the first three verses of Revelation 20, bound the devil. I don't know which one it is. It makes sense either way.

I don't know everything about *The book of Revelation*. A person can teach Revelation even though he doesn't understand every detail about in it. One should not wait until he knows it all. If he waited until he knew it all, he would die first. If you find a teacher of The *book of Revelation* who knows it all, beware of him because God left out some pieces of the puzzle. When Jesus comes again, He is going to put all the pieces together. We can get a good idea what is going to happen. God would not have given the book, if He didn't expect us to study it. However, a few of the pieces are not available.

"He" (the star that falls from heaven) opens the pit or the abyss. Why do I say it might be a heavenly angel? Because he has the key God gave him, the key of the bottomless pit. That is the reason he will be able to put Satan in there and close him up. "And he opened the bottomless pit; and there arose a smoke out of the pit, as the smoke of a great furnace; and the sun and the air were darkened by reason of the smoke of the pit" (Rev. 9:2).

This bottomless pit is the place of confined demons. With that in mind, notice verse 3: "And there came out of the smoke locusts upon the earth: and unto them was given power, as the scorpions of the earth have power" (Rev. 9:3). I am going to call them scorpion locusts because that is what they are. "And it was command-ed them that they should not hurt the grass of the earth, neither any green thing, neither any tree; but only those men which have not the seal of God in their fore-heads" (Rev. 9:4). Who are the ones that have the seal of God on their foreheads? The 144,000. The scorpion locusts are not able to hurt them. Later, John says that the multitude of Gentile believers are also sealed. So the scorpion locusts are not going to hurt anybody who is saved, but they will hurt those who are not saved. Perhaps they will not attack all of the unsaved, but many of them will fall victim to these demonic creatures.

Victims of the scorpion locusts will suffer a prolonged torment. Notice verse 5: "And to them it was given that they should not kill them, but that they should be tormented five months: and their torment was as the torment of a scorpion when he striketh a man" (Rev. 9:5). Five months is the normal time for locusts, from May to September. Their torment was the torment of a scorpion when it strikes a man. Strong men and athletes stung by a scorpion fall down and go into convulsions. Their suffering torments them horribly. Victims are going to be in that type of pain for five months. This period will be one of inescapable torment by demonic creatures unleashed from the bottomless pit. They have power to derange the mind and the body, just like a scorpion does. The Bible says seducing spirits will come.

What does John say about these locusts? "And the shapes of the locusts were like unto horses prepared unto battle; and on their heads were as it were crowns like gold, and their faces were as the faces of men. And they had hair as the hair of women, and their teeth were as the teeth of lions. And they had breastplates, as it were breastplates of iron; and the sound of their wings was as the sound of chariots of many horses running to battle. And they had tails like unto scorpions, and there were stings in their tails: and their power was to hurt men five months. And they had a king over them, which is the angel of the bottomless pit, whose name in the Hebrew tongue is *Abaddon*, but in the Greek tongue hath his name *Apollyon*" (Rev. 9:7-11). Abaddon means "destroyer" and Apollyon means "destroyer." This refers to Satan himself. They are demons because Satan is their king. The Bible says Satan has a kingdom. Jesus says, "How will a kingdom stand against itself?" By speaking these words, He attributes to the devil a kingdom of demons.

There will be demonic activity during the tribulation like there has never been before in the history of the world. The key to the bottomless pit will be used to open it, and out of the abyss will come these demons. They will do to men some-thing like scorpions, but they will come as locusts. The great multitude will stand together covering the world like locusts, but stinging like scorpions.

Angels can manifest themselves and be seen. The fallen angels that are in the abyss are demons. They will possess people and cause convulsions. It probably will be through some things we are going to study later, such as injections, possi-bly narcotics. There will be many narcotics taken during the tribulation. It might be that they will open themselves to demon possession through the injection, which shows how it could be like the sting of a scorpion. Today, many people are demon possessed because they put themselves in the position to be demon possessed through heroin, cocaine, pot, and other narcotics. That is one way a demon can enter, when a person loses control of himself through so-called mind-expanding drugs. Undoubtedly, the tribulation will be a time of terrible possession and affliction.

The first woe has passed and the second woe is yet to come. "One woe is past; and, behold, there come two woes more hereafter" (Rev. 9:12).

The Sixth Trumpet: Demonic Horsemen

Now we come to the sixth trumpet, which is also the second woe, from verses 13 through 21. This is the most terrible judgment encountered so far. "And the sixth angel sounded, and I heard a voice from the four horns of the golden altar which is before God, Saying to the sixth angel which had the trumpet, Loose the four angels which are bound in the great river Euphrates" (Rev. 9:13-14). The voice coming from the altar indicates that the calls for mercy have been rejected from the golden altar. Of course, there was a bronze altar in the temple and the tabernacle, but now in heaven there is a golden altar before God. All of the calls for mercy have been rejected.

The four angels were loosed to bring further judgment upon the earth. "And the four angels were loosed, which were prepared for an hour, and a day, and a month, and a year, for to slay the third part of men" (Rev. 9:15). These angels are bound, so we know they are fallen angels. Heavenly angels are not bound. These are some who fell when they followed the devil, Lucifer, when he fell from his exalted position. They were appointed for a specific hour and a specific day and a specific month and a specific year. They were appointed to be loosed at this precise, particular time. They are going to have power to kill one-third of all mankind. It is going to be a very terrible judgment.

Verses 16 and 17 describe the horses and the horsemen. Evidently they are supernatural, for they are not something we would normally see in this world. "And the number of the army of the horsemen were two thousand thousand (or myriads of myriads); and I heard the number of them" (9:16). The number is Two billion horsemen who are warriors or men on horses. "And thus I saw the horses in the vision, and them that sat on them, having breastplates of fire, and of jacinth, and brimstone (sulfur): and the heads of the horses were as the heads of lions; and out of their mouths issued fire and smoke and brimstone" (Rev. 9:17). Actually, the horses will do the torturing, not necessarily the riders on the horses. This is definitely supernatural.

Notice how the horses torture mankind: "By these three was the third part of men killed, by the fire, and by the smoke, and by the brimstone, which issued out of their mouths" (Rev. 9:18). Three different plagues will be produced by these supernatural horsemen. They have something to do with the four fallen angels who are loosed, probably following after the army of horses. This also has to do with demons because of what we read later. Possibly, this is a human army led by evil spirits. The next verse provides more detail about the torture of the horses. "For their power is in their mouth, and in their tails: for their tails were like unto serpents, and had heads, and with them they do hurt" (Rev. 9:19). It looks as if the tails are like serpents and have heads. That is a peculiar kind of animal that is certainly supernatural.

After one-fourth of mankind died in the first two years of the tribulation (Rev. 6:8), one-third of the remaining will be killed during the next one and a half years (Rev. 9:15) because of this war led by demonic activity. That equals one-half of the world's population.

How will the surviving population respond to this judgment? John says, "And the rest of the men which were not killed by these plagues yet repented not of the works of their hands, that they should not worship devils, and idols of gold, and silver, and brass, and stone, and of wood: which neither can see, nor hear, no walk" (Rev. 9:20). In other words, in that day, even in the Western world there will be idol worship, which is actually demon worship. There is much idol worship in India today. There is a movement today in the Western world, through the "New Age" movement, toward idolatry (demon worship). Men will not repent of this during the tribulation, despite the calamities that happen in the first part of chapter 9 and the more severe judgments that occur in the latter part of chapter 9. God brings all these judgments upon them, but still they refuse to repent.

Notice what will be going on during the tribulation: "Neither repented they of their murders, nor of their sorceries, nor of their fornication, nor of their thefts" (Rev. 9:21). Murder will be very prevalent during the tribulation because of demon worship. Murder is becoming more prevalent today, but during the tribulation murder will become even more widespread. Abortions will be the accepted practice.

In addition to that, witchcraft will also be very widespread. Think about the Harry Potter movement. According to the Bible, idolatry is the worship of demons. The occult, witchcraft, and other things like sorcery are the dynamic of idolatry. In India, the Hindu priests practice witchcraft that is similar to the witchcraft in Africa, Europe and the West Indies, and that of Native Americans. People practice all varieties of witchcraft, which John calls sorcery. They will practice Spiritism. People will try to talk to the dead. Although they may not realize it, these people will actually be talking to demons. Demons are the ones who are talking when they think they talk to the dead. For example, a person named Mr. Jones may be possessed by a demon. When he dies, Mrs. Jones might try to talk to her dead husband. The demon that was in Mr. Jones can imitate Mr. Jones. The demon can actually possess another person who is the contact and talk with the same tones as Mr. Jones. It isn't the man. Rather, it is the demon that was in the man or associated so closely with the man that he knows exactly how he talked. Demons are very powerful. They are more powerful than people realize.

There will be drug addiction because the word translated *sorcery* is actually translated from the word from which we get *pharmacy* or *pharmaceutical*. When you see witchcraft and sorcery in the world, it usually includes narcotics. Narcotics, even today, are used in witchcraft. Magic and astrology are moving towards that. Astrology, Spiritism, black magic, white magic, and drug addiction are all included in the lifestyle of the earth dwellers during the tribulation. One can take drugs without being demon possessed, but with the kinds of drugs they are taking today, a person is in the position to be demon possessed. These mind-expanding experiences put a person in neutral without control of himself. It puts one in a position to yield to demons. That's the reason yoga is very dangerous. It puts a person in neutral, thinking about nothing, and it puts him a position to yield to anything.

Fornication will also be prevalent during the tribulation. God brings all of these judgments upon men because of what they are doing in verse 21. Very few people will get married during the tribulation; they'll just live together. People are moving that way now. Fornication and immorality are rampant on television. People are saying, "What's the purpose of marriage? Why have marriage? It just binds the man, binds the woman, and they don't have freedom." That's what they want more than anything else. They want freedom. There is going to be a breaking down of marriage and the home during the tribulation just like we are seeing even today. The word *fornication* is the translation of the Greek word *porneias*, from which the English gets words beginning with "porn" or "forn." "Porneia" includes pornography, homosexuality (sodomy), incest and child molestation (pedaphilia). All of these immoral acts and life-styles will be legal during The Tribulation. In our day, laws have been moving that way.

Also, there will be much dishonesty. John says, "nor of their thefts." Theft has become widespread in our world today. Consider thefts related to the internet. Also, consider the chief executive officers of large corporations who have been stealing millions.

And so we are seeing a preview in this day of what will occur during the tribulation time: murders, witchcraft, drug addiction, fornication, homosexuality, pedaphilia, living together without being married, and dishonesty.

There are other fallen angels mentioned in Jude who will stay bound continually until the time of the judgment. There are fallen angels that are not bound today. They are demons. But these about which John writes here are bound and will be loosed for a terrible time of demonic activity.

Chapter 16
The Small Scroll and The Two Witnesses
Revelation 10:1 - 11:18

Now we come to another parenthetical vision beginning with chapter 10 and continuing through chapter 11. This parenthetical vision is between the sixth and seventh trumpets.

A Mighty Angel

The first thing we see is another mighty angel. Notice the first seven verses of chapter 10: "And I saw another mighty angel come down from heaven, clothed with a cloud: and a rainbow was upon his head, and his face was as it were the sun, and his feet as pillars of fire" (Rev. 10:1). This is Jesus. He is not one of the four that were bound. This is another strong angel. Notice the phrase "clothed with a cloud." When the Bible mentions clouds, it always refers to a glorious manifestation of the Shekinah glory. This Shekinah glory came into the tabernacle, into the temple, and led the Israelites through the wilderness by day. Jesus was taken up in a cloud. The mention of clouds always relates to God's glory.

Also notice the rainbow on his head. An emerald rainbow encircled the throne. Rainbows symbolize mercy. Therefore, the emerald rainbow represents mercy in the midst of judgment. The rainbow meant mercy in the day of Noah. All of this judgment is going on, but in the middle of it, we see mercy.

This verse likens His face to the sun and his feet to pillars of fire. Revelation 1:15 also depicts Jesus, noting his face was as the sun and his feet were as shining brass, brass that has been in the fire. So this is the Lord Jesus Christ.

The Angel and the Book

What work will this mighty angel perform? "And he had in his hand a little book open...." (Rev. 10:2). This little book is the same little scroll that we read about in chapters 4 and 5. It had seven seals to begin with. Now all of the seven seals have been broken. This little book is the title deed of all the earth. Because Jesus holds the title deed of the earth, He takes possession of the earth and sea by placing His feet on the earth and sea.

Notice verses 2-4: "And he had in his hand a little book open: and he set his right foot upon the sea, and his left foot on the earth, And cried with a loud voice, as when a lion roareth: and when he cried, seven thunders uttered their voices. And when the seven thunders had uttered their voices, I was about to write: and I heard a voice from heaven saying unto me, Seal up those things which the seven thunders uttered, and write them not" (Rev. 10:2-4). Thunder symbolizes judgment. He said, "Don't write those things. Shut them up, seal them up, and don't write them." So he didn't write. When the Lord Jesus spoke, it was like a lion. His words were like the majesty of a lion, the roar of a lion, and then seven thunders. That was judgment. The Lord said, "Don't write those things. Seal it up."

Chapter 10 continues, "And the angel which I saw stand upon the sea and upon the earth lifted up his hand to heaven, And sware by him that liveth for ever and ever, who created heaven, and the things that therein are, and the earth, and the things that therein are, and the sea, and the things which are therein, that there should be time no longer" (Rev. 10:5-6). We see Jesus on the land and on the sea, lifting up His hand to the Father. He says, "There shall be delay no longer." Judgment is going to come! There will be no further delay. This does not mean that time will cease, but that judgment will not be delayed. Verse 7 reemphasizes impending judgment: "But in the days of the voice of the seventh angel, when he shall begin to sound, the mystery of God should be finished, as he hath declared to his servants the prophets" (Rev. 10:7).

What happens to the little scroll? "And the voice which I heard from heaven spake unto me again, and said, Go and take the little book which is open in the hand of the angel which standeth upon the sea and upon the earth. And I went unto the angel, and said unto him, Give me the little book. And he said unto me, Take it, and eat it up; and it shall make thy belly bitter, but it shall be in thy mouth sweet as honey. And I took the little book out of the angel's hand, and ate it up; and it was in my mouth sweet as honey: and as soon as I had eaten it, my belly was bitter. And he said unto me, Thou must prophesy again before many peoples, and nations, and tongues, and kings" (Rev. 10:8-11).

This scroll is the title deed to the world. For the raptured saints of God, the truth that we have title to heaven and things that belong to God is a sweet truth. But for the earth dweller, it will be bitter because it means judgment. It means they are going to have to endure a terrible time of judgment upon the earth. All that belongs to the Lord is certainly wonderful and sweet as honey to those of us who are saved. This indicates grace for those who are saved and judgment for those who are lost. The same gospel, the same message, and the same title deed is gloriously sweet for those who are saved, but terribly bitter to those who are lost.

The Measuring Rod

Chapter 11 records an event that brings joy to think about. "And there was given me a reed like unto a rod: and the angel stood, saying, Rise, and measure the temple of God, and the altar and them that worship therein" (Rev. 11:1). He's given this reed, which is a measuring rod. This was a judicial act to set boundaries.

Especially during Old Testament days, the act of measuring indicated judgment. In this verse, Christ is the measure. All things outside are rejected. Everyone within the boundary is His, but those without are not His. Everyone who participates in the sacrifice of the Lord Jesus Christ, the supreme sacrifice which all other sacrifices foreshadow, is within the boundary. All those without the blood atonement do not belong here. Notice what verse 2 says about those outside the boundary: "But the court which is without the temple leave out, and measure it not; for it is given unto the Gentiles: and the holy city shall they tread under foot forty and two months" (Rev. 11:2). Forty-two months is three and a half years. This is the last half of the tribulation called the Great Tribulation.

The Two Witnesses

In the next part of this parenthetical vision, John sees two witnesses. This is where I really begin to shout. "And I will give power unto my two witnesses, and they shall prophesy a thousand two hundred and threescore days, clothed in sackcloth. These are the two olive trees, and the two candlesticks standing before the God of the earth. And if any man will hurt them, fire proceedeth out of their mouth, and devoureth their enemies: and if any man will hurt them, he must in this manner be killed" (Rev. 11:3 5). Nobody can hurt these two witnesses. They will prophesy three and one-half years, the first half of the tribulation. "These have power to shut heaven, that it rain not in the days of their prophecy: and have power over waters to turn them to blood, and to smite the earth with all plagues, as often as they will" (Rev. 11:6). They will be able to shut up the windows of heaven. For three and one-half years, there will be drought. Think about thousands of forest fires, etc. Also, they will be able to turn water into blood, and smite the earth with every plague as often as they desire.

Who are these witnesses? There are two different views about it. Some people say these two witnesses are Elijah and Enoch. The Bible indicates that when Jesus comes, every believer will be taken up. Yet, there will be two witnesses left or sent back to earth. Some believe that since Elijah and Enoch never died, the two witnesses will be Elijah and Enoch. Others say the witnesses are Moses and Elijah. The Bible prophesies that one like Moses will come and one like Elijah will come, or that Moses and Elijah will come again before Christ sets up His kingdom. Another reason some believe these witnesses are Moses and Elijah is that Elijah shut up heaven so that it would not rain for three and one-half years. Moses turned the water into blood, and called down the plagues on Egypt. Also, Moses and Elijah were at the transfiguration. Therefore, many believe Moses and Elijah are the witnesses.

What is my opinion? I don't know. I'm not sure who they are. I can still understand Revelation, even though I do not understand every detail. That's what I'm trying to get over to you. I do not have to know whether these witnesses are Moses and Elijah, or Enoch and Elijah, or two other witnesses who come in the power of

Moses and Elijah in order to understand that there will be two witnesses. Whether you believe one or the other, there will be two witnesses because the Bible says there will be two witnesses. They will come in the power of Elijah because Elijah shut off the rain for three and one-half years and in the power of Moses because Moses did the very things that one, or both of these witnesses will do.

Notice what happens between the antichrist and these two witnesses, "And when they shall have finished their testimony, the beast that ascendeth out of the bottomless pit shall make war against them, and shall overcome them, and kill them" (Rev. 11:7). The devil, the antichrist, and all their enemies could not touch them until their testimony was finished. I don't care what anyone tries to do to you, dear reader. No one can touch you until your testimony is finished. No government on this earth can do it. No religion can do it. No group of people can do it. No church can do it. No enemy can do it. The antichrist can't do it. Until your testimony is finished, there is no one who can touch you. Isn't that great! If you were one of the only two witnesses in the world, still no one could touch you until God got through with your testimony.

Some ask, "How will the 144,000 Israelites be saved?" We know there will be a multitude of Gentiles saved during the tribulation, people who have never heard the gospel before. They will hear because the 144,000 Israelites will be saved and will become missionaries and witnesses. But how do the 144,000 missionary Israelites get saved? The two witnesses, who are left, proclaim the gospel, bringing the 144,000 Israelites to repentance. Also, Bibles, books (like this one), tracts, audio and video tapes, etc. will be left when the rapture takes place.

What will happen to the two witnesses when their testimony is finished? The antichrist will kill them. "And their dead bodies shall lie in the street of the great city, which spiritually is called Sodom and Egypt, where also our Lord was crucified" (Rev. 11:8). This takes place in Jerusalem because Jesus was crucified in Jerusalem.

"And they of the people and kindreds and tongues and nations shall see their dead bodies three days and an half, and shall not suffer their dead bodies to be put in graves" (Rev. 11:9). How can all people of the earth see these dead bodies? When I was a young college student, some fellows laughed at me and said, "It is impossible for everybody of all nations to see two dead bodies in Jerusalem in three and one-half days." They didn't know about satellite television. Now they can see it through television. The whole world will see them.

"And they that dwell upon the earth shall rejoice over them, and make merry, and shall send gifts one to another; because these two prophets tormented them that dwelt on the earth" (Rev. 11:10). The earth dwellers are going to have a Christmas-like celebration! They are going to have a great big holiday because the two witnesses are dead. They're going to send gifts during this holiday because these two men are dead. But notice what happens. "And after three days and a half the Spirit of life from God entered into them, and they stood upon their feet; and great fear fell upon them which saw them. And they heard a great voice from heaven saying unto them, Come up hither. And they ascended up to heaven in a cloud; and their enemies beheld them" (Rev. 11:11-12). People of the earth will see them come back to life. They still will not repent, even though they see them stand up, come to life again after three and one-half days, and ascend into heaven.

"And the same hour was there a great earthquake, and the tenth part of the city fell, and in the earthquake were slain of men seven thousand: and the remnant were affrighted, and gave glory to the God of heaven" (Rev. 11:13). There is no historical record of this earthquake. This will happen in the future. Those who survive will give glory to the God of heaven, but I'm afraid their praise will be short lived, for they won't repent.

The Seventh Trumpet: Herald of Christ's Coming Kingdom

Notice verse 14: "The second woe is past; and, behold, the third woe cometh quickly. And the seventh angel sounded...." (Rev. 11: 14-15). We have finished the parenthetical portion, and we are gong to see what happens after the seventh trumpet sounds. "And the seventh angel sounded; and there were great voices in heaven, saying, The kingdoms of this world are become the kingdoms of our Lord, and of his Christ; and he shall reign for ever and ever" (Rev.11:15). Here is an announcement of the kingdom. The heavenly voices continue to hail God's greatness: "And the four and twenty elders, which sat before God on their seats, fell upon their faces, and worshiped God, Saying, We give thee thanks, O lord God Almighty, which art, and wast, and art to come; because thou hast taken to thee thy great power, and hast reigned. And the nations were angry, and thy wrath is come, and the time of the dead, that they should be judged, and that thou shouldest give reward unto thy servants the prophets, and to the saints, and them that fear thy name, small and great; and shouldest destroy them which destroy the earth" (Rev. 11:16-18).

Who are the four and twenty elders? All the saints. Here they are giving glory to the Lord because Jesus Christ is about to take over the kingdom upon this earth. It is announced in verse 15. The four and twenty elders proclaim these things that will ultimately happen, but it will be three and one-half years before it will be completed. Throughout the book of Revelation, something is announced in heaven and then it happens on earth. Clearly, Heaven is in control.

In Revelation 11:19, John sees a vision of the open temple, which is an announcement of events to follow. "And the temple of God was opened in heaven, and there was seen in his temple the ark of his testament: and there were lightnings, and voices, and thunderings, and an earthquake, and great hail" (Rev. 11:19). What does that signify? Judgment. Judgment always follows.

Chapter 17
War in Heaven: Satan Cast Out
Revelation 12:1-17

In the next two chapters John describes seven personages. Five of these are seen in Chapter 12.

The Woman With a Crown of Twelve Stars

The first personage is a woman crowned with twelve stars. She is described at the beginning of chapter 12: "And there appeared a great wonder in heaven; a woman clothed with the sun, and the moon under her feet, and upon her head a crown of twelve stars" (Rev. 12:1). This wonder, or sign, meant something. Many times Jesus performed miracles to prove He was the Son of God. The miracles were often called signs.

The woman who appears in this sign represents Israel. In Joseph's dream, he saw twelve stars, a sun and moon. Eleven stars and the sun and moon bowed down to one star. In Joseph's dream, the twelve stars represented the children of Israel. "And she being with child cried, travailing in birth, and pained to be delivered" (Rev. 12:2). As she is about to be delivered, another (second) personage, appears: "And there appeared another wonder in heaven; and behold a great red dragon (dinosaur), having seven heads and ten horns, and seven crowns upon his heads. And his tail drew the third part of the stars of heaven, and did cast them to the earth: and the dragon stood before the woman which was ready to be delivered, for to devour her child as soon as it was born" (Rev. 12:3-4). Who is this dragon? If you look at verse 9, it will tell you. "And the great dragon was cast out, that old serpent, called the Devil, and Satan, which deceiveth the whole world: he was cast out into the earth, and his angels were cast out with him" (Rev. 12:9). The dragon is the devil. He is not the antichrist, but the devil.

Verse 4 says, "And his tail drew the third part of the stars of heaven." What does that mean? Angels. In chapter 1, we find that the stars are angels. Jesus Himself is called "a bright morning star." The word Lucifer means "day star." So when he drew the third part of the stars of heaven and cast them to the earth, what did that mean? Those angels followed him in rebellion and fell with him. Does that mean exactly one-third fell? It could mean exactly one-third, but it could also mean less than one-half. The point is that even if the devil got all but one angel, he cannot win. He can't ever win the battle of the angels because God can create 50 million times more angels than He already has, but Satan can't create anything.

The child to be delivered is the Lord Jesus. Satan, of course, did these things a long time ago. "And the dragon stood before the woman which was ready to be delivered, for to devour her child as soon as it was born. And she brought forth a man child, who was to rule all nations with a rod of iron: and her child was caught up unto God, and to his throne" (Rev. 12:4-5). Of course, the child (the third personage) could have been the antichrist because he is going to rule all nations, or most of them. But when he is caught up to God and to his throne, there is no doubt; this is Jesus. The woman who represents Israel gives birth to Jesus. The devil tried to destroy Jesus, as soon as he was born, when Herod tried to kill Him by killing all babies under two years old. Other times Satan tried to kill Jesus, when they tried to push Him off the cliff at Nazareth, when the Sea of Galilee was storming and the disciples were about to perish, and then when he tried to kill Him in the garden of Gethsemane. Clearly, God delivers. The man child died on the cross, but He was caught up to God. All you have read until now happened in the past. Now John will see something in the future. In the last half of the tribulation, the antichrist will break his treaty with Israel, and he will try to get to her. The devil will try his best to destroy Israel. God will prepare a place of safety, but this doesn't mean that all Israelites will be saved.

Chapter 12 continues, "And the woman fled into the wilderness, where she hath a place prepared of God, that they should feed her there a thousand two hundred and threescore days" (Rev.12:6). The woman will escape and be fed for three and one-half years.

Where is this wilderness? Some think this wilderness is located in Palestine where there are caves for Israelites to hide in. I wouldn't doubt that there will be some of them there. However, there are too many Israelites to be in one particular place. There are Israelites all over the world, even though many of them will have gone back to the land. When he talks about the wilderness, he is talking about more than just that one place where they will go. There will be many of them who will escape to the fringes of society.

War in Heaven

Great war breaks out in heaven as Michael (the fourth personage) and his angels oppose the dragon. "And there was war in heaven: Michael and his angels fought against the dragon; and the dragon fought and his angels and prevailed not; neither was their place found any more in heaven" (Rev. 12:7-8). Before the fall of man, Satan fell from his exalted place. However, he still has access to the Father's throne. Until this time, Satan will have access to the throne to accuse the brethren day and night. This is the reason we need an advocate (attorney) with the Father! But after this defeat, he has no access to the throne to accuse God's children. After this war in heaven, Satan's angels "prevailed not, neither was their place found any more in heaven" (Rev. 12:8).

Once Satan loses his place, he is cast out into the earth. "And the great drag-on was cast out, that old serpent, called the Devil, and Satan, which deceiveth the whole world: he was cast out into the earth, and his angels were cast out with him" (Rev. 12:9). Keep in mind that he is not describing something that has already happened. He is describing a vision. That is the reason he puts this in the past tense. He saw the vision in the past, and he is describing what he saw in the past tense. This is called a prophecy because it is a vision of the future. Satan was cast down to the earth, and his angels were cast down with him. For the last three and one-half years of the tribulation, all of his activity will be limited to the earth.

The Defeated Dragon

The next part of the chapter celebrates the dragon's defeat. Notice verse 10: "And I heard a loud voice saying in heaven, Now is come salvation, and strength, and the kingdom of our God, and the power of his Christ: for the accuser of our brethren is cast down, which accused them before our God day and night" (Rev. 12:10). Right now we have an advocate with our Father, Jesus Christ the right-eous, but one day the accuser of the brethren will be cast down and limited to this earth. He will not have access to the throne to accuse us.

While he accuses, how are they going to overcome? "And they overcame him by the blood of the Lamb, and by the word of their testimony; and they loved not their lives unto the death" (Rev. 12:11). They overcame him using three things: the blood, the word, and their willingness to die. This is how they overcame him, and this is how we can overcome him, too. The thing he hates more than anything else is the blood. He doesn't like preaching on the blood because he despises the blood. Many men are willing to preach on the sufferings of Jesus, but when you begin to talk about the blood, the devil doesn't like it. He wants to take the blood of Christ out of our gospel songs and our teachings.

He also hates the word of their testimony. What is our testimony? The New Testament and the Old Testament are our testimony. That's our contract, our covenant with the Lord. The word of our testimony is based upon the word of God. Friend, if you didn't have the Word of God, you wouldn't have a testimony. Every Christian's testimony is bound up in the Word of God. Satan hates the Word. He tries to destroy the Word. Satan tries to get Bible scholars to teach that the Bible has errors, therefore not inerrant. He tries to destroy the Old Testament and the New Testament, which are the old covenant and the new covenant. He'll never be able to do it. When we stand up to proclaim the Word and give testimo-ny to validate our experience, Satan really hates it. That's what overcomes him: the blood of Jesus and the Word of God. The only offensive weapon we have is the Word of God. When we use the sword of God's Word, the devil will run. We don't throw the Bible at the devil, we quote the Bible.

Also, he hates the principle that we are not afraid of death. While the martyrs were dying, in the early church, people were trusting Christ all over the place. In

China just after the Boxer Rebellion in the 1900s, the massacre of missionaries produced a ten year period when more Chinese were won to Jesus Christ than in the previous century of missionary activity. The blood of the martyrs is the seed of the church. True Christians do not love their lives more than Christ! They are willing to die for Christ. You might never be asked to die; but, even though you are not asked to die physically, you are encouraged to die to self so that the world is dead to you. Paul said he was crucified with Christ, but yet he lived. When you reckon yourself dead and allow Christ to live through you, the devil hates it. This principle of the cross is bound up in the lordship of Jesus. The normal (victorious) Christian life is when you say, "I die to self. Christ is the ruler. He is the lord. He is the sovereign."

The Dragon's Wrath

After being defeated and cast out of heaven, Satan will vent his wrath upon the earth. Verse 12 says, "Therefore rejoice, ye heavens, and ye that dwell in them. Woe to the inhabiters of the earth and of the sea! for the devil is come down unto you, having great wrath, because he knoweth that he hath but a short time" (Rev. 12:12). Notice, Satan knows his end is growing near. Another reason I believe this is in the middle of the tribulation is because of this verse. It will be a horrible time on this earth during those last three and one-half years. It will be the worst time this world has ever known. It will be a very hard time on those who are believers. God will pour out His wrath upon the earth, but Satan in all of his wrath will go after the believers. Notice what happens. "And when the dragon saw that he was cast unto the earth, he persecuted the woman which brought forth the man child" (Rev. 12:13). Who's the woman? Israel. Can he get to her? No.

"And to the woman were given two wings of a great eagle, that she might fly into the wilderness, into her place, where she is nourished for a time, and times, and half a time, from the face of the serpent" (Rev. 12:14). During this three and one-half year period, when the devil unleashes his wrath, the woman will be nourished by God. Also, He is going to give her two wings of a great eagle (fifth personage). What is the great eagle? Some people say it is a jumbo jet. Other people say it is America. Why? The eagle is the symbol for America. What do I think? I'm not sure what the eagle represents. I don't think it is important for me to know exactly what that is. Someday it will be important. For people who read this during the tribulation, it will be important. Right now all I need to know is that she is going to be delivered by the power of God. He is going to provide something symbolized by two wings of an eagle.

We read in the Old Testament how the Lord bears Israel up on eagles' wings. The Lord is going to deliver Israel, whatever He uses. Consider also that God is symbolized by an eagle in the book of Revelation. Remember when we saw the face of a man, the lion, the ox, and the eagle. The eagle we see from

Ezekiel represents a quality of God. This certainly indicates that the Lord himself will do this. The woman is going to be nourished and protected for three and one-half years.

In the next two verses, we see the woman delivered from Satan's assault: "And the serpent cast out of his mouth water as a flood after the woman, that he might cause her to be carried away of the flood. And the earth helped the woman, and the earth opened her mouth, and swallowed up the flood which the dragon cast out of his mouth" (Rev. 12:15-16). Some believe this is literal. They believe the devil is going to cause the antichrist to break a dam and that water will go into an area where Israel is expected to take refuge. Before the water gets to them to destroy them, the earth will open up and the water will go under them instead. Personally, I believe the flood described here is symbolic. It could very well be literal. It is okay with me if it is literal, but I believe Satan is going to use means that will come out of him in order to try to destroy them and that God is going to provide a way for them to be delivered. I do not know whether this is symbolic or literal, but God will not let Satan succeed in his effort to destroy Israel.

Notice Satan's response to defeat: "And the dragon was wroth with the woman, and went to make war with the remnant of her seed, which keep the commandments of God, and have the testimony of Jesus Christ" (Rev. 12:17). Who is the remnant of her seed? The remnant is the 144,000. These are the Israelites who keep the commandments of God and have the testimony of Jesus. Who among Israel will trust Jesus as Savior? The 144,000. So what is the devil going to do? He is going to begin to persecute the 144,000 saved and witnessing Israelites. What did we write previously that their logical response would be? They are going to scatter. They are going to try to get away. Where are they going? To the fringes of civilization where many people can hear the gospel and be saved, because they have never heard the gospel before.

Next, we'll study in more detail about the antichrist.

Chapter 18
Satan Worship and the Mark of the Beast
Revelation 13:1-18

There is disagreement among conservatives about the beast of the earth and the beast of the sea. Some believe that the beast out of the earth is the antichrist. They believe the beast out of the sea is the empire. I believe that the beast out of the sea is the empire, but the antichrist is part of that empire. He becomes the main ruler and is the personification of the empire. He is the anointed, of the devil. In the word *antichrist*, the word *Christ* does not mean "savior," it means "anointed one." The word *Jesus* means "savior." The antichrist does not have to come from the Jewish tradition. He will forsake the religion of his fathers, which could be any form of religion. I believe the beast out of the earth is the false prophet.

The Beast of the Sea: The Antichrist

Beginning with Revelation 13:1, we see a beast coming out of the sea (the sixth personage). This vision deals with the ten kingdom empire. This ten kingdom empire is typified by the beast, and the imperial head of the empire is the antichrist. Behind it all is Satan, who will be worshiped directly during these days. John says, "...and I stood up on the sand of the sea and I saw a beast." In this chapter, the word *beast* is not the same word that we find in the sixth chapter, where it is a living creature. Here *beast* refers to a hideous kind of beast, like a wild beast. John said, "I saw a beast coming out of the sea." When something comes out of the sea and not out of the land, it has to do with Gentiles. This terrible beast will come out of the Gentiles, not out of Israel.

The verse continues, "... having ten horns and seven heads, and on his horns ten diadems, and upon his heads names of blasphemy" (Rev. 13:1). This empire is typified by the beast, and each of the heads of the beast is one of the successor kingdoms that we can read about in Daniel. He is the same one we find in Revelation 17:3-17. This is the one that supports and carries the harlot who typifies the apostate religion. This woman is a prostitute sitting upon a scarlet-colored beast full of the names of blasphemies, having seven heads and ten horns. This beast will be a reconstituted government or the reinstatement of the Roman empire. Even as this book is being published, there are nations related to a union in Europe that could very well be the beginning of this ten kingdom empire, ruled by Satan through the antichrist.

In the second chapter of Daniel, we see a prophesy that came from the dream of King Nebuchadnezzar. Daniel interpreted the dream and indicated that God was prophesying that there would be four great kingdoms. The first would be Babylon ruled by Nebuchadnezzar, the second would be Medea-Persia, the third would be Greece, and the fourth would be Rome. Then the chapter talks about the Lord Jesus Christ, the stone made without hands, who would finally overcome the world government and set up his own kingdom.

The beast out of the sea, described in Revelation 13, is very similar to the four beasts in Daniel 7. In Daniel 7, the four beasts came up out of the sea, which indicates they were Gentiles. One was like a lion, one was like a bear, one was like a leopard, one was very terrible and dreadful. Likewise, Revelation 13 describes a beast with the characteristics of a leopard, a lion, a bear, and a dragon. Evidently, this beast is the same as the beasts we see in Daniel. The beast represents the different kingdoms in the world. These will be successive kingdoms, but the last kingdom will have certain qualities that are found in all the other kingdoms. The second verse of chapter 13 reads, "And the beast which I saw was like unto a leopard, and his feet were as the feet of a bear, and his mouth as the mouth of a lion; and the dragon (the devil himself according to the twelfth chapter of Revelation) gave him his power, and his throne, and great authority" (Rev.13:2).

This beast with ten horns and seven heads represents the great empire or dictatorship that will come during the tribulation period. The seven heads symbolize the seven successive empires of this world. The dragon (Satan) has always given power to these kingdoms. The ten horns, with crowns, symbolize the ten leaders of the ten governments that will make up the reconstituted Roman Empire.

In verse 3 John writes, "And I saw one of his heads as though it had been smitten unto death (the Greek word means "slain"); and his death stroke (plague) was healed: and the whole earth wondered after the beast" (Rev.13:3). One of the heads, which will be the world empire led by the antichrist, will receive a death-blow. It will seem as if the antichrist dies, but he will be healed of this death stroke. Because the world thinks that he was raised from the dead, the whole earth will be amazed by the beast. However, this apparent resurrection will be a lying wonder because he will not actually be raised from the dead.

This seeming miracle will cause the world to give adoration to the beast and also to the dragon who gives power to the beast. In verse 4 we read, "And they worshiped the dragon (that is the devil), because he gave his authority (power) unto the beast; and they worshiped the beast saying, Who is like unto the beast? And who is able to make war with him?" (Rev. 13:4). Satan worship will be established during the tribulation through the devil giving authority in supernatural power to the antichrist. Notice then the blasphemies of the beast found in verse 5. It states, "And there was given to him (to the antichrist) a mouth speaking great things and blasphemies; and there was given to him authority to continue forty and two months (Rev. 13:5). This means he will rule, by Satan's power for three and one-half years, the last half of the tribulation period.

The book of Daniel also mentions the blasphemies prophesied in verse 5. Daniel says:

> And the King shall do according to his will; and he shall exalt himself, and magnify himself above every god, and just speak marvelous things against the God of gods and shall prosper till the indignation be accomplished; for that that is determined shall be done. Neither shall he regard the God of his fathers nor the desire of women nor regard any god for He shall magnify himself above all. And in his estate shall he honor the god of forces and a god whom his fathers knew not shall he honor with gold and silver and with precious stones and pleasant things. Thus shall He do in the most strong holds of a strange god whom He shall acknowledge and increase with glory and he shall cause them to rule over many and shall divide the land for gain (Daniel 11:36-39).

The main feature of this rule will be blasphemies against God, against His name, against the tabernacle (which is His dwelling place), and even them that dwell in heaven (See Rev. 13:6).

According to verse 7, there will be universal rule of the beast, who is the antichrist. John says, "And it was given unto him to make war with the saints and to overcome them; and there was given to him authority (power) over every tribe and people and tongue and nation" (Rev.13:7). Daniel 7:25 states, "And He shall speak great words against the most High, and shall wear out the saints of the most High, and shall think to change times and laws: and they shall be given into his hand until a time and times and the dividing of times" (which means three and a half years).

Daniel 9:27 indicates something about a covenant he makes with Israel but later breaks: "And he shall confirm the covenant with many for one week (which means seven years): and in the midst of the week (after three and one-half years) he shall cause the sacrifice and the oblation to cease, and for the overspreading of abominations he shall make it desolate, even until the consummations and that determined shall be poured upon the desolate." This verse indicates that the antichrist will make a covenant with Israel for seven years, but in the middle of that seven years he will break the covenant.

He will set himself up to be god and to be worshiped in the temple of God. (See II Thess. 2.) He will make people worship him and his image all over the world. Actually, this will be the worship of Satan himself. The dragon will be worshiped according to Revelation 13:4. Verse 8 indicates that the whole world will worship the beast, the antichrist: "And all that dwell on the earth (the earth dwellers, not those who are sealed by the seal of God) shall worship him, every one whose name hath not been written from the foundation of the world in the book of life of the Lamb that hath been slain" (Rev. 13:8).

Earth dwellers (those who have not been saved) will worship the antichrist. Through the antichrist, they will be worshiping the dragon, who is the devil. The only way they will be able to buy or sell will be to worship the antichrist.

The world religion will be destroyed at this time even though it is an apostate, or false religion, so that all earth dwellers will be worshiping the antichrist. Verses 9 and 10 contain an exhortation to hear an important statement. There is divine retribution indicated but also help for the saints, indicating that they should be steadfast.

The Beast of the Earth: The False Prophet

The latter part of chapter 13 deals with the religious leader or the minister of religion, who will be given authority by the antichrist. His job will be to give testimony about the antichrist and to encourage people to worship him. Now let us look at this second beast (seventh personage) that comes out of the land, indicating that he will come out of Israel. He will be Jewish. "And I beheld another beast coming up out of the earth; and he had two horns like a lamb, and he spake as a dragon" (Rev. 13:11). This verse doesn't say he was a lamb. Some think this is the antichrist because it says "he had two horns like a lamb." But it doesn't say he was like a lamb, or trying to act like Jesus, the lamb. Rather, his horns are like a lamb's horns, and he spoke as a dragon. His authority, symbolized by his horns, was like a lamb's authority. Thus, his authority was some kind of religious authority. But he spoke in the power of the dragon, or in the power of the devil.

Verse 12 explains his mission: "And he exerciseth all the power of the first beast before him, and causeth the earth and them which dwell therein to worship the first beast, whose deadly wound was healed" (Rev. 13:12). So he had the same authority as the antichrist. Verses 13 and 14 indicate that the minister of religion, or false prophet, has power to work miraculous signs. "And he doeth great wonders, so that he maketh fire come down from heaven on the earth in the sight of men, And deceiveth them that dwell on the earth by the means of those miracles which he had power to do in the sight of the beast; saying to them that dwell on the earth, that they should make an image to the beast, which had the wound by a sword, and did live" (Rev. 13:13-14).

The devil, the antichrist, and the false prophet comprise an unholy trinity. The devil is the father of lies. The antichrist is the lie. The false prophet gives testimony and witness about the antichrist. On the other hand, The Father, Son, and Holy Spirit comprise the holy trinity. God the Father is the Father of the truth. Jesus Christ, the Son, is the truth, the incarnation of the Lord God. The Holy Spirit gives testimony to and for the Lord Jesus Christ. The Holy Spirit gives testimony to Christ, and Christ gives honor to the Father. In the unholy trinity, the false prophet gives testimony to and about the antichrist and causes people to worship him. The antichrist gives glory to the father of lies who is the devil, Satan himself.

The Mark of the Beast

Verse 15 further describes the power of the false prophet: "And he had power to give life unto the image of the beast, that the image of the beast should both speak, and cause that as many as would not worship the image of the beast should be killed" (Rev. 13:15). The antichrist will be the worldwide ruler, and people will worship him. If they don't, the false prophet will see to it that they are killed.

Also, the false prophet will mandate the mark of the beast. "And he causeth all, both small and great, rich and poor, free and bond, to receive a mark in their right hand, or in their foreheads: And that no man might buy or sell, save he that had the mark, or the name of the beast, or the number of his name. Here is wisdom. Let him that hath understanding count the number of the beast: for it is the number of a man; and his number is Six hundred threescore and six" (Rev. 13:16-18). That mark of the beast will be the name of the beast or the number of his name. In order for a person to be able to buy or sell anything, he must have the mark of the beast on his forehead or on his hand. Why? When people walk into a store, the mark of the beast will be evident. Or when they sign something like a credit card slip, the mark of the beast will be evident on their hands.

The mark of the beast is not in this age. It will be in the age of the tribulation. This is an example of how the mark will be used. Have you ever had a mark on your hand? Have you ever gone to Six Flags or Disney Land? If you leave, but want to return, the attendants mark something on your hand. Why? Because when you go back through, they could put it under an ultraviolet ray or another kind of light and they could see the mark, and let you return. It isn't seen in regular light, but it is seen when it is put under the special light. It would be very easy to set up a system so that every time a person walks into a room, into a store, or into an arena, a special light would hit him to indicate whether he had the mark of the beast. Also, a smaller special light could be installed over the place where a person would sign his name. People will be required to have the mark of the beast in order to buy and sell.

How does one get the mark of the beast? He has to worship the beast, or his image. If one doesn't worship the beast or his image, he can't get the mark. If one doesn't have the mark, he can't buy anything. If one does have the mark, if one does worship the beast, he is lost. Anyone who is saved will not worship the image. The people who are saved, the 144,000, and the multitudes of Gentiles who trust the Lord as Savior during the tribulation will not be able to buy and to sell. They will have to find some other way to find food. The Bible indicates that no one who receives the mark of the beast will be saved. We'll see that later.

What is the mark? Verse 18 answers this question. "Here is wisdom. Let him that hath understanding count the number of the beast: for it is the number of a man; and his number is Six hundred threescore and six" (Rev. 13:18). In other words, his number is 6 6 6. What does it mean? What is the number 6? It is the number of man. So what is the Lord saying? He is a man, he is a man, he is a man. He is not God. If you are trying to figure out who he is, you will never do it because he will not be revealed until there is a great going away, until the church is taken out. If you figure out who he is, that means you've been left behind.

The beast is a man. He is not a nation. He is not the ten nations that will make up the revived Roman Empire. He is not the common market. He is a man, he is a man, he is a man. He is not God; he is a man. That is another reason I do not believe that the first beast out of the sea is merely the nation. He is the antichrist who is the personification of an empire, and he is a man.

Next, heaven indicates that there will be a bloody Battle of Armageddon.

Chapter 19
A New Song and Pure Wrath
Revelation 14:1-20

In spite of all the ugliness we have seen in the first and second parenthetical passages, we see a beautiful picture of something in heaven in this third parenthetical passage. Peace is just ahead — the millennial bliss that is coming one day. In chapter 14, we see the power of God in intervention. Grace and judgment are manifested here.

The Lamb and the 144,000

Chapter 14 begins, "And I looked, and, lo, a Lamb stood on the Mount Zion and with him an hundred forty and four thousand, having his Father's name written on their foreheads" (Rev. 14:1). The Lamb is the Lord Jesus, of course. Mount Zion is the place of the millennial throne. The 144,000 saints have the Father's name written on their foreheads, not the name of the beast. In other words, they give testimony that they worship the Lamb, the Lord Jesus Christ who is standing on Mount Zion, the place where the millennial throne will be. We see here a picture of the future kingdom. John is looking past the tribulation in this vision.

Let's look at the 144,000. "And I heard a voice from heaven, as the voice of many waters, and as the voice of a great thunder: and I heard the voice of harpers harping with their harps" (Rev. 14:2). We find out in Chapter 15 exactly who they are. They are those who are martyred in the tribulation. These martyrs are harping with their harps. That's how people got the idea that when a person dies, he's going to play a harp. These are the ones who play a harp, but the song they sing, no one else can sing. Verse 3 says, "And they sung as it were a new song before the throne, and before the four beasts, and the elders: and no man could learn that song but the hundred and forty and four thousand, which were redeemed from the earth" (Rev. 14:3).

There are four things we can say about the 144,000. First, they were confessors of Christ. That's found in the first verse, "having his Father's name written in their foreheads." In the third verse we see that they are unworldly because "they sung as it were a new song before the throne." The 24 elders are actually in a better position. We are represented by the 24 elders, but now these are before the throne and they sing a new song before us, for verse 3 says, "... and before the four beasts, and the elders." They are the only ones to perform this particular work during the tribulation period. They were Jews who were saved during the tribulation, and no one else can sing their song. It is a song of grace to be sure, but it is a song that only they could sing. We cannot sing that song. We will not be in the tribulation. The multitudes of Gentiles who are saved cannot sing that song. They are not the chosen witnesses, the 144,000 precious witnesses who are Jewish believers during the tribulation.

Secondly, they have been purchased out of the earth. Verse 3 also says, "... and no man could learn that song but the hundred and forty and four thousand, which were redeemed from the earth." They are not of the world, and they are purchased out of the land (earth). The Greek word can be translated either "earth" or "land." The "land" is what JHWH had promised Abraham - the promised land. These are Israelites.

The third thing we see about the 144,000 is found in verse 4. Here we see that they are pure. "These are they which were not defiled with women; for they are virgins. These are they which follow the Lamb whithersoever he goeth." (Rev. 14:4). They are virgins. Of course, a man can be a virgin. In a terrible time of tribulation when everyone seems to be participating in fornication and very few people marry, they remain pure. They probably will not marry. If they marry, this means they are virgins when they marry. If they remain unmarried, they remain pure. Whether they marry or not, they will be pure. They will be virgins. They will not participate in the fornication that will be the very spirit of the age of the tribulation when so many people forsake even the idea of marriage. These follow the Lamb. What happens when you follow the Lamb? Jesus said; "Follow me and I'll make you to become fishers of men." Aren't they going to be witnesses? He promises a reward if you follow. If you are a witness, you'll receive the crown of a witness.

The 144,000 were the first ones saved during the tribulation. "These were redeemed from among men, being the first fruits unto God and the Lamb." Jesus is the first fruit of the first resurrection, but these are the first fruits of those saved during the tribulation. Therefore, they will be saved before the Gentiles. Not only are they pure, but the fourth thing we can say about them is that they are truthful and honest in deed as well as in word. Verse 5 says, "And in their mouth was found no guile: for they are without fault before the throne of God" (Rev. 14:5). They can be accused of no lie in word, and they are without blemish even in deed.

The Proclamation of the Eternal Gospel

The first thing we dealt with in this chapter was the Lamb on Zion and the 144,000. Now we are going to deal with the proclamation of the eternal gospel. The proclamation, praise the Lord, is that the tribulation is almost over. Verses 6 and 7 state, "And I saw another angel fly in the midst of heaven, having the everlasting gospel to preach unto them that dwell on the earth, and to every nation, and kindred, and tongue, and people, Saying with a loud voice, Fear God, and give glory to him; for the hour of his judgment is come: and worship him that made heaven, and earth, and the sea, and the fountains of waters" (Rev. 14: 6-7). The angel is in mid-heaven, or in the air.

What is this eternal gospel? Do not get me wrong, I know that Paul said, "As we have said before, so I say again now, if any man is preaching to you a gospel contrary to that which you received, let him be accursed" (Gal. 1:9). He was talking about the good news of how to be saved. The word translated "gospel" is the Greek word "<u>evangel</u>," which means "good news," or "good message." There are many good tidings. But this good tiding is found in the fact that judgment of God is just about to come, and all of this tribulation time will be complete. The Lord is about to come in judgment and, praise God, all of the horrors of the tribulation will be over.

In verse 8 another angel continues the good news. "And another angel, a second one, followed, saying 'Fallen, fallen is Babylon the great, she who has made all the nations drink of the wine of the passion of her immorality' " (Rev. 14:8). This is the third part of the "good news." Babylon is fallen. This could also be part of the eternal gospel. It's an announcement of what will be seen in detail in chapters 17 and 18. We will discover in chapters 17 and 18 that Babylon is a religion. That which happens on earth was already announced in heaven!

The Wrath of God

Now we come to another section of this chapter, the eternal wrath of God for the worshipers of the beast. "And the third angel followed them, saying with a loud voice, If any man worship the beast and his image, and receive his mark in his forehead, or in his hand, The same shall drink of the wine of the wrath of God, which is poured out without mixture into the cup of his indignation; and he shall be tormented with fire and brimstone in the presence of the holy angels, and in the presence of the Lamb" (Rev. 14:9-10). This will be true wrath because there won't be any dilution of it at all. It is going to be the pure wrath of God prepared unmixed for those who worshiped the beast or his image, and therefore received the mark on their forehead or on their hand.

Verse 11 portrays the terrible torment prepared for those who bow to the antichrist. "And the smoke of their torment ascendeth up for ever and ever: and they have no rest day nor night, who worship the beast and his image, and whosoever receiveth the mark of his name" (Rev. 14:11). Those who take the easy route of embracing the antichrist during the tribulation will suffer unimaginable, unrelenting torment for all eternity. On the other hand, those who choose the hard route of rejecting the antichrist will be rewarded for their steadfastness. Notice verse 12: "Here is the patience of the saints: here are they that keep the commandments of God, and the faith of Jesus." (Rev. 14:12). The word *patience* means "steadfastness." It is going to take steadfastness for saints (holy ones) to go through the tribulation. Verse 13 pronounces blessing upon those who are steadfast throughout the tribulation. "And I heard a voice from heaven saying unto me, Write, Blessed are the dead which die in the Lord from henceforth: Yea, saith the Spirit, that they may rest from their labours; and their works do follow them" (Rev. 14:13). Blessed are those who die in the Lord. Preachers use this verse in funerals. Of course, it is applicable. Everyone who dies in the Lord, even in this day, is *blessed*. However, in the tribulation, some saints will be happy to die. The word blessed means "to be made happy." They are going to cease from their labors and from all tribulation when they die. This verse specifically refers to those who die during the tribulation period. They are very blessed when they die from this point on because they will be resting from their labors.

The Harvest of the Earth

The remainder of chapter 14 focuses on the harvest and vintage, which lead to the Battle of Armageddon. "And I looked, and behold a white cloud, and upon the cloud one sat like unto the Son of man, having on his head a golden crown, and in his hand a sharp sickle" (Rev. 14:14). This is the Lord. The cloud indicates glory. He has the golden crown indicating his kingship, but in his hand a sharp sickle. Why is He carrying a sickle? "And another angel came out of the temple, crying with a loud voice to him that sat on the cloud, Thrust in thy sickle, and reap: for the time is come for thee to reap; for the harvest of the earth is ripe" (Rev. 14:15). The sickle deals with reaping of the earth. Most who will be on the earth at that time will be lost people who have worshiped the image of the beast. "And he that sat on the cloud thrust in his sickle on the earth; and the earth was reaped" (Rev. 14:16).

The last four verses of chapter 14 vividly predict and describe the harvest and the subsequent bloodbath resulting from the Battle of Armageddon. "And another angel came out of the temple which is in heaven, he also having a sharp sickle. And another angel came out from the altar, which had power over fire; and cried with a loud cry to him that had the sharp sickle, saying, Thrust in thy sharp sickle, and gather the clusters of the vine of the earth; for her grapes are fully ripe. And the angel thrust in his sickle into the earth, and gathered the vine of the earth, and cast it into the great winepress of the wrath of God. And the winepress was trodden without the city, and blood came out of the winepress, even unto the horse bridles, by the space of a thousand and six hundred furlongs" (Rev. 14:17-20). That is 200 miles. God's judgment and wrath will cause the blood to flow to the horses' bridles for 200 miles at the Battle of Armageddon. At places it will be four and one-half feet high. One commentator indicates this could be the splashing of blood. He could be right, but the blood could just as well flow that high. The bodies of those who are part of the armies of the antichrist could burst, and the blood flow that high.

Let's find out more about the unholy trinity.

Chapter 20
The Seven Last Plagues
Revelation 15:1-16:21

Prelude to the Seven Plagues

Chapters 15 and 16 are about the "seven angels having the seven plagues" in "bowls of wrath." "And I saw another sign in heaven, great and marvelous, seven angels having the seven last plagues; for in them is filled up the wrath of God" (Rev. 15:1). John had been seeing several signs. As far back as the twelfth chapter, he'd been seeing signs.

Now he sees another sign in heaven. It seems as if the wrath of God is going to be completely spent upon the earth. There will be no more after this. It is almost time for peace on the earth. It is almost time for the Lord Jesus Christ to come in glory. These are the last plagues. The seven seals have been opened, and the seven trumpets have sounded. Now the seven angels will pour out the vials of wrath of the plagues. We are still under the seventh seal and we are still under the seventh trumpet. What comes out of that are the seven plagues.

John sees another scene in heaven, one altogether different. "And I saw as it were a sea of glass mingled with fire: and them that had gotten the victory over the beast, and over his image, and over his mark, and over the number of his name, stand on the sea of glass, having the harps of God. And they sing the song of Moses the servant of God, and the song of the Lamb, saying...." (Rev. 15:2,3). These who have the harps and sing are the 144,000. They are worshiping the Lord in heaven. This is a picture of what happens after the tribulation, after the plagues are finished.

Again, this is a vision in heaven about what is about to happen later on earth. These are those who are victorious over the beast and over his image. They did not worship his image, nor did they receive the number of his name. They are standing on the sea, and they sing the song of Moses. They are the 144,000, for only Israelites could sing the song of Moses. They also sing the song of the Lamb, so they have to be saved. The saved Israelites, the 144,000, are going to be singing this song. Part of the song will be these words: "Great and marvelous are thy works, Lord God Almighty; just and true are thy ways, thou King of saints. Who shall not fear thee, O Lord, and glorify thy name? for thou only art holy: for all nations shall come and worship before thee; for thy judgments are made manifest." (Rev. 15:4).

In verses 5 through 8, John sees the seven angels proceeding out of the temple of the sanctuary in heaven. "And after that I looked, and behold, the temple of the tabernacle of the testimony in heaven was opened" (Rev. 15:5). This is the point of operations for their coming to pour out the wrath of God upon the earth. In verse 6, we see these angels dressed in priestly garments. "And the seven angels came out of the temple, having the seven plagues, clothed in pure and white linen, and having their breasts girded with golden girdles" (Rev. 15:6). This is the way a priest would be clothed. The reason they are clothed in that way is because they are God's representatives doing this in the name of God. "And one of the four beasts gave unto the seven angels seven golden vials (bowls) full of the wrath of God, who liveth for ever and ever" (Rev. 15:7). The bowls come from the Lord, from one of the living creatures representing the characteristics of God. He gives to the angels these golden vials, these golden bowls, full of God's wrath.

Now we see the Shekinah glory of the LORD, but it's not the same kind of Shekinah glory that we've seen before when the Lord filled the tabernacle and the temple. "And the temple was filled with smoke from the glory of God, and from his power; and no man was able to enter into the temple, till the seven plagues of the seven angels were fulfilled" (Rev. 15:8). Remember when the Shekinah glory of JHWH came into the tabernacle. It was in a cloud. Remember in the days of Solomon, the Shekinah glory of God came into the temple. It was symbolized by a cloud. Now we don't see a cloud, but we see smoke. It also relates to the glory of God, for it says, "the temple was filled with smoke from the glory of God, and from his power." When you see the cloud, that indicates grace. When you see the smoke, that indicates judgment, for smoke comes from the altar and that's the place of judgment. John sees the sanctuary of heaven filled with the smoke of the glory and power of God. This indicates so much judgment that no one was able to enter into the sanctuary until the seven plagues of the seven angels were finished.

Another reason the angels are dressed in priestly garments is that they do the work of a priest before the Lord in the sanctuary in heaven. This is a vision of the things that are happening in heaven. The sanctuary represents the meeting place where we meet with the Lord and where we can have fellowship with God. The sanctuary is a dedicated place where, because of the sacrifice of the Lord Jesus Christ, we can have fellowship with God. The reality behind the picture is more important than the picture itself. Even though the temple or tabernacle was a literal thing that you could see and touch, at the same time all the parts of that tabernacle had a symbolic meaning that was far more important. Jesus is the supreme sacrifice. It is through His blood we can have a wonderful experience of fellowship with the Lord. That's the main thing. Maybe when we get to heaven, there will be an actual sanctuary. However, I would rather have fellowship with the Lord Jesus Christ and the Father through Him instead of going through the ritual of having a sanctuary like they had in the days of Moses and the days of the law. Praise the Lord, we're under grace.

The smoke fills the temple until the judgment is complete. John sees what these vials, or bowls, hold as they are poured out. "And I heard a great voice out of the temple saying to the seven angels, Go your ways, and pour out the vials of the wrath of God upon the earth" (Rev. 16:1). This voice comes from the sanctuary. I don't know whose voice it is. It could be the voice of God. It could be the voice of one of the four living creatures because the four living creatures were the ones that gave to the seven angels the seven golden bowls full of the wrath of God. However, the four living creatures represent the attributes of God, so it is the voice of God, in either case.

The First Vial: Grievous Sores

Notice the first bowl in verse 2. Also, notice all these plagues come from heaven. "And the first went, and poured out his vial upon the earth; and there fell a noisome and grievous sore upon the men which had the mark of the beast, and upon them which worshiped his image" (Rev. 16:2). This appears to be the same thing that happened in Egypt during the plagues. The sixth plague upon the Egyptians was boils or grievous sores. Exodus 9 illustrates the similarity of these plagues. "And the LORD said unto Moses and unto Aaron, Take to you handfuls of ashes of the furnace, and let Moses sprinkle it toward the heaven in the sight of Pharaoh. And it shall become small dust in all the land of Egypt, and shall be a boil breaking forth with blains upon man, and upon beast, throughout all the land of Egypt" (Ex. 9:8-9). When this happens during the tribulation, it will not be upon beasts. It will be only on mankind. "And they took ashes of the furnace, and stood before Pharaoh; and Moses sprinkled it up toward heaven; and it became a boil breaking forth with blains upon man, and upon beast. And the magicians could not stand before Moses because of the boils; for the boil was upon the magicians, and upon all the Egyptians. And the LORD hardened the heart of Pharaoh, and he hearkened not unto them; as the LORD had spoken unto Moses" (Ex. 9:10-12).

This is like the plague that came upon Egypt. Keep in mind that the Bible says that some of the plagues of Egypt will come in the last days. And so, here are some of them. Why do people have boils? Bad blood. It is corruption in the blood. This is actually very symbolic of real corruption in the hearts of the people. It might be something related to the worship of the antichrist. All those will have boils who worship the image of the beast. Every one of them. The people who don't worship his image will not have the boils. Those who are saved, those who refuse to bow down, will not have boils.

Therefore, the boils actually symbolize the spiritual corruption in them. It might be that this will be caused by what they participate in as they worship the beast. Also, it might be that because the tribulation saints can't buy and sell, they won't be able to buy some of the items the antichrist's followers can buy and eat and drink. The boils may be the result of what they eat and drink, and their blood will cause the boils to come forth. I don't know what is going to cause the boils, but I know it's going to happen during the tribulation. These sores could be cancer!

This plague will literally come to pass. It literally came to pass in the days in Egypt. This is not a figurative thing. John doesn't say "likened to" like he says in the second verse of chapter 15: "I saw as it were a sea," indicating that this particular passage is figurative, since he says "as it were." Nothing like that is said in the sixteenth chapter. Because it happened in Egypt, I believe it will happen worldwide in the days of the antichrist, in the days of the tribulation just before the Lord comes. In forty-two months all these things will happen. These seven plagues will come in three and one-half years, the last part of the tribulation. Like pharaoh, the earth dwellers will harden their hearts. Remember, this plague will be only on those who worship the beast.

The Second Vial: Seas Become Blood

Now let's look at the second vial, or bowl. "And the second angel poured out his vial upon the sea; and it became as the blood of a dead man; and every living soul died in the sea" (Rev. 16:3). The phrase *living soul* means "conscious life." The whole of the sea is affected here. Part of the sea is affected when the seals are opened. That will happen in the first three and one-half years, but it will get worse, not better. It will get so bad that everything in the sea, all of the living creatures, the conscious life in the sea, will die because the water will become as the blood of a dead man. The chemical make-up of the sea (with salty water) is very similar to the content of human blood. It will be a horrible time. They talk about pollution today and about the seas dying. They talk about the Gulf of Mexico perhaps dying in the next few years. It will take very little to change the sea to be like blood. This plague could be a result of man's pollution.

The Third Vial: Fresh Waters Become Blood

The vial of the third angel also affects the waters. "And the third angel poured out his vial upon the rivers and fountains of waters; and they became blood. And I heard the angel of the waters say, Thou art righteous, O Lord, which art, and wast, and shalt be, because thou hast judged thus. For they have shed the blood of saints and prophets, and thou has given them blood to drink; for they are worthy. And I heard another out of the altar say, Even so, Lord God Almighty, true and righteous are thy judgments" (Rev. 16:4-7). They are getting what they have deserved. Because they poured out the blood of saints and prophets, they will have blood to drink. This is like the first of the Egyptian plagues found in Exodus 17. This could be a result of pollution.

The Fourth Vial: Scorching Fire

In Chapter 8, the fourth angel sounds his trumpet, bringing darkness upon the earth. "And the fourth angel sounded, and the third part of the sun was smitten, and the third part of the moon, and the third part of the stars; so as the third part of them was darkened, and the day shone not for a third part of it, and the night likewise" (Rev. 8:12). That will happen during the first part of the tribulation, but we see something quite different in chapter 16. "And the fourth angel poured out his vial upon the sun; and power was given unto him to scorch men with fire" (Rev. 16:8). These men will be scorched by the heat of the sun. That is quite different from what we find in the trumpets judgment. Could this be the result of the destruction of the ozone layer?

Malachi 4 prophesies this event depicted in Revelation 16. "For, behold, the day cometh, that shall burn as an oven; and all the proud, yea and all that do wickedly, shall be stubble: and the day that cometh shall burn them up, saith the LORD of hosts, that it shall leave them neither root nor branch. But unto you that fear my name shall the Sun of righteousness arise with healing in his wings; and ye shall go forth, and grow up as calves of the stall" (Mal. 4:1-2). Who is the Sun of righteousness? Christ is the Sun of righteousness. The prophecy in Malachi points to the latter days. In Revelation, John reports that he sees a vision of this prophecy fulfilled.

"And men were scorched with great heat, and blasphemed the name of God, which hath power over these plagues: and they repented not to give him glory" (Rev. 16:9). Just exactly like Pharaoh, they will harden their hearts. Instead of repenting and giving God glory, they blasphemed His name, even though He was the one who had power over them. This heat will cause the snow on the mountains to melt. The ice on both North and South poles will melt, at least partially. Waters will partly cover cities. Also, Noah's ark will be visible on Mt. Ararat. However, earth dwellers will still not repent.

The Fifth Vial: Darkness in the Beast's Kingdom

Look at the fifth plague upon the earth during the great tribulation. "And the fifth angel poured out his vial upon the seat of the beast; and his kingdom was full of darkness; and they gnawed their tongues for pain" (Rev. 16:10). The seat of the beast will probably be Babylon. There will be little electricity because not any water will be left in the rivers. The mountains' ice caps will have melted and passed on to the sea. Therefore, the kingdom will be full of darkness. There will be no air-conditioning. People will gnaw their tongues in pain — pain from the scorch of heat, but darkness will also come upon them. There will be many complete blackouts.

Instead of crying to God in repentance, they blaspheme Him. "And blasphemed the God of heaven because of their pains and their sores, and repented not of their deeds" (Rev. 16:11). They still have the sores. Everything in the sea is dead, and they are drinking bloody water or water that is like blood. Now they are scorched, and there is darkness over the face of the kingdom of the beast. Still they will not repent. They harden their hearts just like Pharaoh did. These things will come one right after another. They don't get over one plague before another comes rapidly upon them. All these last plagues could be caused by man's pollution.

The Sixth Vial: The Euphrates Dried Up

The sixth vial is poured out. "And the sixth angel poured out his vial upon the great river Euphrates; and the water thereof was dried up, that the way of the kings of the east might be prepared" (Rev.16:12). This is literal. The Red Sea was literally dried up, and the Israelites went across on dry ground. The Jordan River was also literally dried up. First it was done to deliver the children of Israel from Pharaoh. Then it was done to take them into the land of Canaan. Now, it will be done in order to get these Christ-hating armies over into Megiddo so they might be trapped and killed when the Lord Jesus Christ comes in His glory. The Euphrates River will be dried up by the same power by which the Red Sea was parted. No rain for the first half of the tribulation, plus the melting of most ice caps will cause the Euphrates to be dry.

Next comes a parenthetical vision, but it does relate to verse 12. These kings of the sun rising are not necessarily from the immediate East. The land of the rising sun is really the literal interpretation. There is a land of the sun rising. It might be Japan or it might be Iran (Persia) Iraq, Pakistan, Saudi Arabia and all the nations now influenced by Al-Qaida. It's going to be from the East. There will be several nations come from the East. Also there will be some come from the South.

In verse 13, we see the unholy trinity again. "And I saw three unclean spirits like frogs come out of the mouth of the dragon, and out of the mouth of the beast, and out of the mouth of the false prophet" (Rev. 16:13). The dragon is the devil. The beast is the antichrist. The false prophet is the religious leader. Here is the unholy trinity, three of them together. The three frogs represent evil spirits who are demons. "For they are the spirits of devils, working miracles, which go forth unto the kings of the earth and of the whole world, to gather them to the battle of that great day of God Almighty" (Rev. 16:14). The demon spirits will come out of the unholy trinity: the devil, the antichrist, and the false prophet. The demons will convince the kings of the East that they should come together to fight against Israel. God is the first cause in bringing them there, allowing this to happen in order that He might destroy them. These will be lying spirits, deceiving spirits, deluding spirits. They will be what Paul calls "seducing spirits" in I Timothy. They will want to destroy Israel. Of course, the main purpose of God will be to get these kings to gather together in battle. When that happens, the Lord will come and destroy them.

Notice verse 15: "Behold I come as a thief. Blessed is he that watcheth, and keepeth his garments, lest he walk naked, and they see his shame" (Rev. 16:15). Jesus says not only to watch, but to keep his garment. "And he gathered them together into a place called in the Hebrew tongue Armageddon" (Rev. 16:16). These judgments will happen. God will cause them to happen.

The Seventh Vial: An Earthquake and Hail

The seventh angel pours out his vial in verse 17. "And the seventh angel poured out his vial into the air; and there came a great voice out of the temple of heaven, from the throne, saying, It is done" (Rev. 16:17). The seventh vial actually is under the seventh trumpet, which is under the seventh seal. When the voice says, "It is done," that means that this is the end of all the plagues upon the earth. Finally, it is the end.

"And there were voices, and thunders, and lightnings; and there was a great earthquake, such as was not since men were upon the earth, so mighty an earthquake, and so great" (Rev. 16:18). The first time, under the seventh seal, John heard only thunders. Then under the seventh trumpet, he heard voices, thunders, and hail stones. He sees a little bit in the seals, then he sees more in the trumpets, and then he sees a great deal more in the plagues, or the vials. So he is seeing more each time. This is how the Book of Revelation progresses. Verse 17 says, "It is done." This means the wrath of God is finished. All He has started in heaven will now be accomplished on earth. In other words, all of this is under the seventh seal, under the seventh trumpet, under the seven vials. God's wrath will still be seen on earth, but the announcing of all his wrath has now come to an end.

The first vial does not come after the last trumpet. The vials come "out of" the seventh trumpet. He gives John more and more and more as each one of these visions is seen. In the seals John sees what will happen. In the trumpets John sees more that will happen. In the vials, a fuller view of what will happen is seen. In other words John receives a progressive vision.

John sees a panoramic view of the entire seven years. We can be sure that certain things happen during the first three and one-half years, such as the antichrist coming on the scene. Other things definitely happen during the last three and one-half years. Some of it could happen either time or both times.

Verse 19 continues to portray God's judgment upon earth. "And the great city was divided into three parts, and the cities of the nations fell: and great Babylon came in remembrance before God, to give unto her the cup of the wine of the fierceness of his wrath" (Rev. 16:19). John sees another thing that is going to happen on earth that he has not seen before. Yet, it had been announced in heaven. "And every island fled away, and the mountains were not found" (Rev. 16:20). In other words, they were just flat. This could be the result of a great earthquake.

"And there fell upon men a great hail out of heaven, every stone about the weight of a talent: and men blasphemed God because of the plague of the hail; for the plague thereof was exceeding great" (Rev 16:21). A talent is about 100 pounds. The word translated "hail" is the Greek word "lithinos," which means "rock." This hail out of heaven could be a great volcanic eruption or meteorites. Still, right here at the very end, they do not repent.

The Revelation of Jesus Christ

Zechariah 14 describes the revelation of Jesus Christ. "And his feet shall stand in that day upon the mount of Olives, which is before Jerusalem on the east, and the mount of Olives shall cleave in the midst thereof toward the east and toward the west, and there shall be a very great valley; and half of the mountain shall remove toward the north, and half of it toward the south. And ye shall flee to the valley of the mountains; for the valley of the mountains shall reach unto Azal: yea, ye shall flee, like as ye fled from before the earthquake in the days of Uzziah king of Judah: and the LORD my God shall come, and all the saints with thee" (Zech. 14:4-5). This occurs at the time of the revelation of Christ. Look at verses 10 and 11 "All the land shall be turned as a plain from Geba to Rimmon south of Jerusalem: and it shall be lifted up, and inhabited in her place, from Benjamin's gate unto the place of the first gate, unto the corner gate, and from the tower of Hananeel unto the king's winepresses. And men shall dwell in it, and there shall be no more utter destruction; but Jerusalem shall be safely inhabited" (Zech. 14:10-11). This is a prophecy of a time of peace, Judah will be turned into a virtual garden.

Other scriptures also verify it is going to be a wonderful, beautiful place. Look at Ezekiel 47:1. "Afterward he brought me again unto the door of the house; and, behold, waters issued out from under the threshold of the house eastward; for the forefront of the house stood toward the east, and the waters came down from under, from the right side of the house, at the south side of the altar" (Ezek. 47:1). Verse 8 adds, "Then said he unto me, These waters issue out toward the east country, and go down into the desert, and go into the sea: which being brought forth into the sea, the waters shall be healed" (Ezek. 47:8).

"But the miry places thereof and the marshes thereof shall not be healed; they shall be given to salt" (Ezek. 47:11). In this forty-seventh chapter of Ezekiel, we also see a prophecy of this same time, evidently. It looks as if there is going to be a catastrophic event that is going to change the earth geologically. Maybe an earthquake is going to come, and the Mount of Olives will break into two parts by this earthquake. In addition, the entire city will be torn into three parts. The mountains will be brought low, and there will be wonderful fields. There are areas of the Holy Land that used to be rocky, desert places but now they are being farmed because of irrigation. They are now being turned into beautiful places where they raise good food. However, at the end of the tribulation, through this great earthquake, there will come a time when mountains will be made flat and Judah will be turned into a habitable plain. According to the Old Testament, they will be able to farm it all, and it will be wonderful.

There never was a harlot like the one we are about to see.

Chapter 21
The Horrible Harlot
Revelation 17:1 - 18

In chapter 17, John describes a vision of the judgment of Babylon the great harlot. Here we begin dealing with seven dooms or judgments, and this is the first of the seven. These seven judgments will be punishment upon the Satanic trilogy. The first four of these come before the millennium. The last three of these come after the millennium.

Description of the Woman

In the first six verses, John describes a woman. This is mystical Babylon, the great harlot. "And there came one of the seven angels which had the seven vials, and talked with me, saying unto me, Come hither; I will show unto thee the judgment of the great whore that sitteth upon many waters: With whom the kings of the earth have committed fornication, and the inhabitants of the earth have been made drunk with the wine of her fornication" (Rev. 17:1-2). The angels have already poured out their bowls. John then is shown the judgment upon a woman who is called a harlot. She had intimate spiritual relations with the kings of the earth, and the kings of the earth committed fornication with her. They that dwell upon the earth were made drunken with the wine of her adultery, her fornication, and her unfaithfulness. That means the earth dwellers have been affected by the unfaithfulness of this woman.

"So he carried me away in the spirit into the wilderness: and I saw a woman sit upon a scarlet coloured beast, full of names of blasphemy, having seven heads and ten horns" (Rev. 17:3). The scarlet color means it is bloody. This beast upon which she sits is the same beast that we have seen before in chapter 13, but now we are going to get a fuller picture of this particular beast. Now we see the color. The beast himself is full of the names of blasphemy. We see the progression from this beast that blasphemes against God, but now everyone involved in the worldwide kingdom of the beast, will be full of blasphemy.

The woman was sitting upon this beast, so the woman, who is the Babylonian religion, will be supported by the revived Roman Empire. During the first half of the Tribulation, this reestablished Roman empire, headed by the antichrist, will completely support the Babylonian New Age religion. The seven successive world empires have always supported the woman (the Babylonian religion).

"And the woman was arrayed in purple and scarlet colour, and decked with gold and precious stones and pearls, having a golden cup in her hand full of abominations and filthiness of her fornication" (Rev. 17:4). She has great riches, and she will be arrayed in beautiful garments and pearls. In her hand she holds a cup full of abominations, indicating idolatry. We see in the cup the unclean things of her fornication. These unclean things include the heresies, the idolatry, the occult, and the mystical things that have to do with demons and Satan in that cup.

Identity of the Woman

Verse 5 identifies the name of the wicked woman portrayed in chapter 17. "And upon her forehead was a name written, MYSTERY, BABYLON THE GREAT, THE MOTHER OF HARLOTS AND ABOMINATIONS OF THE EARTH" (Rev. 17:5). Babylon is the bride of the antichrist, just as the church is the bride of Christ. This is not a literal city in chapter 17, but an apostate system that began with Nimrod and finally became the Babylonian religion and influenced the church. This is Babylon, which is the mother of harlots (apostate churches and other religions).

If we are to understand Babylon, we have to go back to the tower of Babel, which was erected in the days of Nimrod. The city of Babylon was right on the banks of the Euphrates River, which also ran through the original Garden of Eden. It goes back a long way. It might be that Satan actually had his headquarters there when he was about to tempt Adam and Eve. But we know that after the flood, the tower of Babel was built. Evidently those who did not follow Jehovah God gravitated there.

We find, in secular history, that Nimrod established a kingdom where he was not only king, but also high priest; and his wife/mother was the high priestess. When Nimrod's father died, his young mother was afraid that she would be overthrown; therefore, she said that the baby who was to be born was actually the father reincarnated in her. When Nimrod was born she raised him and married him. This is from secular history. There were many pictures of the Madonna and a child centuries before Jesus Christ was born. The worship of the Madonna and the child was not a worship of Mary and Jesus Christ to begin with. It started when this queen had a son. By the way, Cupid in Greek mythology relates to the old high priestess and child. There are teachings (or myths) in the Hindu religion that relate to this "goddess and child." All the false religions of the world have elements of the Babylonian religion in them.

Nimrod started this mystical brotherhood. Witchcraft, Spiritism, and astrology were introduced to the world by this religion. The high priest ruled over everyone, not only as a civil king, but also religiously as a high priest. A person had to renounce allegiance to his family and give all allegiance to the "mystical brotherhood" of the Babylonian religion in order to be a member of this cult. Centuries later the kingdom of Babylon fell to Persia, the high priest of the Babylonian religion went to Pergamos, where it was in John's lifetime. The king of Pergamos was then the Pontiff of the cult. At the death of Attalus, the king of Pergamos, in 133 B.C, the headship of the Babylonian priesthood was given to Rome. Julius Caesar was made Pontiff in 74 B.C. From that time on, the emperors of Rome were also the high priests who were worshiped. All this came from an unbroken line that goes all the way back to Nimrod.

All other pagan religions in the world have been influenced by this Babylonian religion. Every religion in this world, except true Christianity, has been influenced by the Satanic religion of Babylon. The Roman Catholic religion has much of the Babylonian religion with a good portion of Christianity mixed in. In A.D. 376, a Roman emperor named Gratian refused to accept this high priesthood because of Christian reasons. Therefore, Damasius, the bishop of Rome, was elected to the position of Supreme Pontiff in A.D. 378. This united Rome and Babylon into one religion. From that time, the worship of Mary began. The use of the rosary and the festivals of Babylon began to creep into the Roman Catholic Church from the Babylonian religion. All these things originated in Babylon. Easter is the name of the Babylonian goddess Ishtar, (Ashteroth in the Old Testament). The sign of the cross was the sign of TAU, which is the Greek letter T, the first letter of the word *TAMMUZ*. This was used for magical purposes in the Babylonian religion centuries before Christ. It can be found numerous times in I and II Kings and I and II Chronicles because many of the people of Israel worshiped Ashteroth.

From the day of Nimrod, the religion of Jehovah has been attacked by the religion of Babylon, which is the religion of Satan. The religion of Babylon has always been at war with the saints throughout history. It became worldwide at the confusion of the tongues when people left Babylon. The throne has been moved from Babylon to Pergamum and then to Rome.

Just as Christ has the church as His bride, the antichrist also has a bride. His bride is the religion of Babylon. After the rapture, all religions will revert back to the old Babylonian religion with all of its ceremony, its relation to demons, and the worship of Satan. All religions will go back to the old religion started by Nimrod. The present day New Age religion has most of the beliefs of the Babylonian religion. After the rapture, it will be easy for most earth dwellers to embrace the New Age. The kings have been drunk on her fornication, and the people of the earth have, too. The ecumenical movement will be complete. This is not merely one church, but one religion. Apostate Christianity will unite with all other religions of the world. Diversity!!!!

Now the greatest evidence that this religion is actually of the devil is found in verse 6. "And I saw the woman drunken with the blood of the saints, and with the blood of the martyrs of Jesus: and when I saw her, I wondered with great admiration (amazement)" (Rev. 17:6). In other words, he wondered greatly. Babylon is not a literal city here, but an apostate system. At this time in the tribulation, it will carry the people of the world back to the beginning of false worship. This religion will be carried along on the back of the beast. The Babylonian religion will be supported by the beast, the antichrist and his empire.

The Babylonian religion was headed by the emperors of Rome in John's day, and many saints were killed by them. All the persecution and martyrdom were caused by those who were head of the Babylonian religion at that time. Later through the Inquisition, many were martyred because of the "church," after the head of the church of Rome also became the head of the Babylonian religion. During the tribulation, this intensified effort to kill those true believers will be continued, from what we see in the sixth verse. There will be an accelerated effort for a worldwide religion. They will increasingly incorporate the things of Babylon as all apostate churches identify more and more with all other religions during the Tribulation.

Mystery of the Woman

Verse 7 gives the interpretation by the angel. "And the angel said unto me, Wherefore didst thou marvel? I will tell thee the mystery of the woman, and of the beast that carrieth her, which hath the seven heads and ten horns. The beast that thou sawest was, and is not; and shall ascend out of the bottomless pit, and go into perdition" (Rev. 17:7-8). This beast that was and is not and is about to come up is the Roman Empire because the Roman Empire was, but now it is not, but it will be again during the tribulation. It will come up out of the abyss and finally go into perdition. Verse 8 continues, "...and they that dwell on the earth shall wonder, whose names were not written in the book of life from the foundation of the world, when they behold the beast that was, and is not, and yet is" (Rev. 17:8). The beast here and in chapter 13 represents the revived Roman Empire. It will be led by the antichrist. The antichrist is synonymous with this beast, and is the dictator of the revived Roman Empire.

"And here is the mind which hath wisdom. The seven heads are seven mountains, on which the woman sitteth" (Rev. 17:9). Most of the time in apocalyptic literature, mountains represent government. Some people think this is Rome, but Rome isn't on seven mountains. Many commentaries teach that this is Rome because Rome is a city of seven hills. But so is Lynchburg, Virginia. "And there are seven kings: five are fallen, and one is, and the other is not yet come; and when he cometh, he must continue a short space" (Rev. 17:10). There are seven kings in verse 10, and there are ten kings in verse 12, so we have to understand which is which.

"And the beast that was, and is not, even he is the eighth, and is of the seven, and goeth into perdition" (Rev. 17:11). John said seven, then eight. "And the ten horns which thou sawest are ten kings, which have received no kingdom as yet; but receive power as king one hour with the beast" (Rev. 17:12). So John sees seven kings, then an eighth king, then ten kings. The seven kings are successor empires beginning with Nimrod in Babylon. Different nations took over the authority of government that supported this religion going all the way back to

Nimrod. This was not necessarily one man as a king, but successive orders of government supported by Satan. In verse 9, John finds that seven heads are seven mountains on which the woman sits. Five of them had already fallen and one is. That is Rome. The other yet to come is the revived Roman Empire, which will continue a little while. The revived Roman Empire, as it is taken over by the antichrist, is the eighth. The ten horns are the ten kings or kingdoms that are established under this Roman Empire at the time it is revived. What about the ten kings, what about the common market, and now the European Union, and the fact that the Union has three cities where the government of Europe meets? There will be ten kings. Three of them will be deposed, and the antichrist will come up to replace those three. That will come after the rapture, but a close observer of times and events can see how it could happen soon.

The kings of the revived Roman Empire will support the antichrist. "These have one mind, and shall give their power and strength unto the beast. These shall make war with the Lamb, and the Lamb shall overcome them: for he is Lord of lords, and King of kings: and they that are with him are called, and chosen, and faithful" (Rev. 17:13-14).

"And he saith unto me, The waters which thou sawest, where the whore sitteth, are peoples, and multitudes, and nations, and tongues. And the ten horns which thou sawest upon the beast, these shall hate the whore, and shall make her desolate and naked, and shall eat her flesh, and burn her with fire" (Rev 17:15-16). These rulers will hate this religion that they have supported so long. So she will become desolate and naked. This will happen in the middle of the tribulation period.

God actually uses these wicked rulers to accomplish His ultimate plan. "For God hath put in their hearts to fulfill his will, and to agree, and give their kingdom unto the beast, until the words of God shall be fulfilled. And the woman which thou sawest is that great city, which reigneth over the kings of the earth" (Rev. 17:17-18). Why do the antichrist, the false prophet, and the kings of the earth hate her? Because in the middle of the tribulation, the antichrist decides that he wants to be worshiped. He becomes Satan incarnate, and Satan longs for this worship. He had been getting some of it through the Babylonian religion, but in the middle of the tribulation, the antichrist will establish himself as God to be worshiped as God. That's the reason he forsakes this religion and condemns it. Therefore, he destroys this Universal State Religion, which is the Babylonian religion. Apostate churches (including Roman Catholicism), and other religions, are merely the daughters of the great whore, not the harlot herself. The demonic religion started by Nimrod, is that great prostitute.

Could the next chapter be a double prophecy?

Chapter 22
The Fall of Babylon
Revelation 18:1 - 24

Revelation 18 begins by portraying the ultimate fall of Babylon. "And after these things I saw another angel come down from heaven, having great power; and the earth was lightened with his glory. And he cried mightily with a strong voice, saying Babylon the great is fallen, is fallen, and is become the habitation of devils, and the hold of every foul spirit, and a cage of every unclean and hateful bird" (Rev. 18: 1-2). Many conservatives take this to be mystical Babylon, or the Babylonian religion. The worship of idols and the practice of idolatry leads to possession by demons. The power behind those images, is the power of demons. The demons will do things for the idolator only if he yields more and more to the demon, until the demon has total control. All religions — Buddhism, Taoism, Hinduism, and apostate Christianity — have become a habitation of demons and every unclean spirit and every unclean and hateful bird. This will be an evil, heretical system.

The prophesy in Zechariah 5 talks about two women. They are going to be carried by a stork, which is an unclean bird in the Old Testament law. If one identifies these birds in verse 2 with that stork, then he will come to the conclusion that literal Babylon could be rebuilt during the tribulation. If the Lord tarries, it could be rebuilt even in our day. If Jesus came today, it would take only five years to build a city like that.

The City of Babylon

Old Babylon was 15 miles square. It had 250 towers along the walls. It had a wall that was 87 feet thick and 350 feet high, which is 50 feet higher than the length of a football field. Six chariots could go abreast on the top of the wall. They had 25 large avenues that went north and south, and 25 large avenues that went east and west. They met each other diagonally, which created 676 square blocks in the city of Babylon.

The city was divided into two equal parts by the Euphrates River. There were steps down to the river. At the end of the bridge over the river, there was a palace, where there were ways to go underneath the ground and even underneath the river. They had great banquet halls down there. That is where Belshazzar was having his great feast during the time that he was defeated. At the end of the major avenues, they had gates made of brass. They were called gates of flame.

The tower of Babel was 660 feet high above the wall. That's more than twice the length of a football field. It was actually eight towers, one upon the other. This tower was a temple for worship. They used it to worship the planets and to practice astrology. They had one golden idol which was worth seven million dollars in that day. Of course, it would be worth much more today. The utensils they used in worship were worth two million dollars in that day.

There is a real possibility that literal Babylon will be rebuilt, and some conservative scholars believe it will. They believe that the prophesy in Isaiah 13 has not yet been fulfilled. Isaiah prophesied that Babylon will be devoid of humans and become like Sodom and Gomorrah. This has not happened yet. It is to happen in "the day of the Lord." Babylon has not yet been cast into the Euphrates River (See Jer. 51:63). Possibly, Babylon will be rebuilt by the antichrist before the horrible events take place. Those conservative scholars believe Babylon is a literal city to be restored and then destroyed, and the religion came out of the city.

The Religion of Babylon

Verse 3 says, "For all nations have drunk of the wine of the wrath of her fornication, and the kings of the earth have committed fornication with her, and the merchants of the earth are waxed rich through the abundance of her delicacies" (Rev. 18:3). Merchants have gotten rich by selling and providing for these Babylonian religions like Hinduism, Taoism, Buddhism, and apostate Christianity. According to secular history, Nimrod started his religious state because of his desire for riches and luxuries. Also, Nebuchadnezzar brought Babylon to its heights through greed and power. All through history, and even now, the power of the world is under the control of international financiers who manipulate governments. Keep in mind the oil of Iraq is located near the site of ancient Babylon.

Next comes a call to God's people to separate themselves from the apostate system. "And I heard another voice from heaven, saying, Come out of her, my people, that ye be not partakers of her sins, and that ye receive not of her plagues. For her sins have reached unto heaven, and God hath remembered her iniquities" (Rev. 18:4-5). Those who are saved during the tribulation are called to reject the Babylonian religion. The only person who can be saved during the tribulation is one who never heard nor rejected the gospel before Christ comes for us. When they trust the Lord, they will come out of her. This includes those who come out of idolatry and the New Age religion. They will not participate in her sins nor her plagues. This could also mean the city of Babylon. During the tribulation, the few who have been saved will be encouraged to come out of the city upon which judgment is about to come.

Notice how Babylon will be rewarded for her wickedness. "Reward her even as she rewarded you, and double unto her double according to her works: in the cup which she hath filled, fill to her double" (Rev. 18:6). She is going to receive double for what she did. She did many things to true churches and to Christians throughout history. Babylon has killed the prophets. Jezebel killed the prophets. In the last 100 years, more Christians have been martyred than in all previous ages. In the last seventy years, Babylon has martyred many in Columbia, Spain, India, Sudan, the Middle East and South America. For example, they tried to kill evangelist Anibal Reis in Brazil because he had been a Roman Catholic priest. Once he was saved, he came out from among them and began to preach the gospel. They repeatedly tried to kill him but they failed. She is going to receive double according to her works.

"How much she hath glorified herself, and lived deliciously, so much torment and sorrow give her: for she saith in her heart, I sit a queen, and am no widow, and shall not see sorrow" (Rev. 18:7). She is going to receive according to her luxury. Babylon, the city, will receive all the judgment that God pours out on the rest of the earth, plus the plagues of the sixth trumpet and the fifth and sixth bowls. Her judgment will be sudden, according to verse 8. "Therefore shall her plagues come in one day, death, and mourning, and famine; and she shall be utterly burned with fire: for strong is the Lord God who judgeth her" (Rev. 18:8). She is going to fall suddenly.

Kings Mourn Babylon's Fall

Those who basked in her luxuries will mourn her fall. "And the kings of the earth, who have committed fornication and lived deliciously with her, shall bewail her, and lament for her, when they shall see the smoke of her burning, Standing afar off for the fear of her torment, saying, Alas, alas that great city Babylon, that mighty city! for in one hour is thy judgment come" (Rev. 18:9-10). It is going to be sudden, like the destruction of the twin towers of the World Trade Center on September 11, 2001. Those who believe it is a literal city rebuilt, say that this will be happening just as in the days of Noah, that people will be marrying and giving in marriage. All of a sudden in one hour, this will come. "And the merchants of the earth shall weep and mourn over her; for no man buyeth their merchandise any more" (Rev. 18:11). What is this merchandise? The merchandise of the apostate churches, the merchandise of all the religions that are part of Babylon. If you study idolatrous worship in Hinduism, you will see that it is a merchandise. It's something you receive by performing something or by paying something.

No man will buy their merchandise anymore. "The merchandise of gold, and silver, and precious stones, and of pearls, and fine linen, and purple, and silk, and scarlet, and all thyine wood, and all manner vessels of ivory, and all manner vessels of most precious wood, and of brass, and iron, and marble, And cinnamon, and odours, and ointments, and frankincense, and wine, and oil, and fine flour, and wheat, and beasts, and sheep, and horses, and chariots, and slaves, and souls of men" (Rev. 18:12-13). She has received these things through the years, and in return she has given indulgences and many other things.

Of course, those who believe it will be a rebuilt literal city believe all this will literally happen, especially when one reads the middle and end of verse 13, which says, "... and wheat, and beasts, and sheep, and horses, and chariots, and slaves, and souls of men." This Babylon of chapter 18 may be the literal city, which started and developed the Satanic religion that has covered the world since the confusion of tongues. "And the fruits that thy soul lusted after are departed from thee, and all things which were dainty and goodly are departed from thee, and thou shalt find them no more at all. The merchants of these things, which were made rich by her, shall stand afar off for the fear of her torment, weeping and wailing, And saying, Alas, alas, that great city, that was clothed in fine linen, and purple, and scarlet, and decked with gold, and precious tones, and pearls!" (Rev. 18:14-16). Of course, this could be the literal city, but also this is true about these false religions, related to Babylon. "For in one hour so great riches is come to nought. And every shipmaster, and all the company in ships, and sailors, and as many as trade by sea, stood afar off, And cried when they saw the smoke of her burning, saying, What city is like unto this great city!" (Rev. 18:17-18).

Those who mourn the fall of Babylon will weep and wail, according to verse 19. "And they cast dust on their heads, and cried, weeping and wailing, saying, Alas, alas, that great city, wherein were made rich all that had ships in the sea by reason of her costliness! for in one hour is she made desolate" (Rev. 18:19). Notice after the mourning comes the rejoicing of heaven in verse 20. "Rejoice over her, thou heaven, and ye holy apostles and prophets; for God hath avenged you on her" (Rev. 18:20).

Total Destruction of Babylon

Verse 21 portrays the total destruction of Babylon. "And a mighty angel took up a stone like a great millstone, and cast it into the sea, saying, Thus with violence shall the great city Babylon be thrown down, and shall be found no more at all" (Rev. 18:21). That's the reason they relate this particular prophecy to Zechariah and Isaiah, where it was prophesied that Babylon would be found no more. The prophecy certainly is to be fulfilled in the future. She will be found no more.

It is hard to determine whether this is the literal city or mystical Babylon. The whole idea of Babylon is that is was this terrible religion. It was built as a defiance against God by Nimrod and then the descendants of Nimrod. Babylon itself is not so much the city of brick walls as it is the world system of religion. At the time when the languages were confused by the Lord and they scattered, this horrible religion scattered all over the world and infected many people. However, it might be that a literal city of Babylon will be put under the sea because of an earthquake and the melting of the ice caps caused by the prophesied heat.

"And the voice of harpers, and musicians, and of pipers, and trumpeters, shall be heard no more at all in thee; and no craftsman, of whatsoever craft he be, shall be found any more in thee; and the sound of a millstone shall be heard no more at all in thee" (Rev. 18:22). Those who believe that this is a literal city say this is the kind of thing that will be going on. The inhabitants will be dancing. Also they will have the minstrels, the theaters, the trumpeters, the rock bands, and so forth. All of this will stop. At the same time, these details could support the belief that Babylon is a mystical city. False religions that came out of the old Babylonian religion have these same things. Throughout history they have been noted for this very thing. Today, in America, those who practice the New Age religion are in business and commerce. The other Babylonian religions like Hinduism have the same.

All light and joy will cease. The city will become a place of darkness and doom. "And the light of a candle shall shine no more at all in thee; and the voice of the bridegroom and of the bride shall be heard no more at all in thee: for thy merchants were the great men of the earth; for by thy sorceries were all nations deceived. And in her was found the blood of prophets, and of saints, and of all that were slain upon the earth" (Rev 18:23-24). This could be true about mystical Babylon or a literal city. The sorceries by which all the nations were deceived is the Babylonian religion, not just the city. The influence of Babylon on the world through sorcery, black magic, Spiritism, astrology, has been tremendous. Finally, look at the blood of the saints found in her in verse 24. That is another reason I tend to believe that it is mystical Babylon. We do have New Testament prophets. The prophets definitely were slain, as well as the saints, in the days of Jezebel who was a priestess of the Babylonian religion.

Chapter 17 is a prophecy about mystical Babylon, which is the religion started by Nimrod and scattered all over the world to infiltrate and influence all religions, even what is now apostate Christianity. During the first half of the tribulation (perhaps even before the rapture), it will become the state religion. It will be the old religion of Nimrod, but under a new name, such as New Age. By its nature, it can incorporate all religions, except true Christianity. Could that be the reason for the attacks on true evangelical Christians, who believe there is one way of salvation, which is by trusting in the only begotten Son of God, who died on the cross to bare our sins and was raised from the dead?

The city of Babylon has never been completely destroyed as the Old Testament prophets foretold. The city could very well be the center of the worship of the antichrist during the last half of the tribulation. It could also be the center of commerce, communication. It could be the world capitol of the antichrist. Chapter 18 could be a double prophecy (as many prophecies are) of the city as symbolic of the religion. Both will be destroyed.

Now, Christ is about to come in glory!

Chapter 23
The Marriage of the Lamb and Revelation of Christ
Revelation 19: 1 - 21

The Four-fold Alleluia

In the first ten verses of chapter 19, John describes the four-fold alleluia and the marriage of the Lamb. "And after these things I heard a great voice of much people in heaven, saying, Alleluia; Salvation, and glory, and honour, and power, unto the Lord our God" (Rev. 19:1). This is after the announcement of the destruction of Babylon. Immediately after that, in heaven, there is a great alleluia, which means "praise the Lord."

In the Old Testament, the word *alleluia* is found 24 times. Every time it is translated "praise the Lord." In the New Testament it is found only four times. All four times are found in this passage, the only place in the Bible where the word is not translated. It is transliterated "alleluia" or "hallelujah." Either way, it means "praise the Lord."

The first alleluia continues in verse 2. "For true and righteous are his judgments: for he hath judged the great whore, which did corrupt the earth with her fornication, and hath avenged the blood of his servants at her hand" (Rev. 19:2). There will be a time during the tribulation when vengeance will come. Those in heaven will cry out for vengeance and praise God for the vengeance He sends. The second alleluia comes in verse 3. "And again they said, Alleluia. And her smoke rose up for ever and ever" (Rev. 19:3). The smoke from Babylon goes up eternally.

Those around the throne say the third alleluia in verses 4 and 5. "And the four and twenty elders and the four beasts fell down and worshiped God that sat on the throne, saying, "Amen; Alleluia. And a voice came out of the throne, saying, Praise our God, all ye his servants, and ye that fear him, both small and great" (Rev. 19:4-5). Since the voice comes from the throne, this indicates that the voice is from the Lord. He says, "Give praise to our God." It could be from the Lamb because it comes from the throne.

Next comes the fourth alleluia. "And I heard as it were the voice of a great multitude, and as the voice of many waters, and as the voice of mighty thunderings, saying, Alleluia: for the Lord God omnipotent reigneth" (Rev. 19:6). When you see "as it were," it is always symbolic. He didn't hear the actual voice of waters, but it sounded like many waters.

The Bride Made Ready

Verse 7 moves away from glorifying God for the destruction of the harlot. Now the praise focuses on the Lamb coming to wed His bride. "Let us be glad and rejoice, and give honour to him: for the marriage of the Lamb is come, and his wife hath made herself ready" (Rev. 19:7). John sees the Lamb about to marry the true bride of Christ who has made herself ready. How was she made ready? During the tribulation period, the church will stand before the judgment seat of Christ.

Paul wrote about the judgment seat of Christ in 2 Corinthians 5:10. He says we must all stand before the judgment seat of Christ that we may receive everything done in our bodies according to that which we have done, whether it be good or bad. The basis of that judgment is found in 1 Corinthians:

> For no man can lay a foundation other than the one which is laid, which is Jesus Christ. Now if any man builds upon the foundation with gold, silver, precious stones, wood, hay, straw, each man's work will become evident; for the day will show it, because it is to be revealed with fire; and the fire itself will test the quality of each man's work. If any man's work which he has built upon it remains, he shall receive a reward. If any man's work is burned up, he shall suffer loss; but he himself shall be saved, yet so as through fire (1 Cor. 3:11-15).

All of us try to do good works. All of us do works that might seem good. These are going to be evaluated one day. Everything Christians have done will be evaluated.

This will not be the judgment when all who are lost are going to stand before the great white throne. During the time of the tribulation, the raptured saints will stand in heaven before the judgment seat of Christ. The purpose of this judgment is to evaluate our works, not to determine whether we go to heaven or hell. The child of God will never be judged according to his works. If he were judged according to his works, he would go straight to hell. However, his works will be judged to determine his reward in heaven. He will be completely purged. The church is not fit now to be the wife of the Lord. However, when the church gets through this time of purging at the judgment seat of Christ, when all of the bad things are burned up, she will be prepared. That's what it means here when it says, "Let us be glad and rejoice, and give honour to him: for the marriage of the Lamb is come, and his wife hath made herself ready" (Rev. 19:7).

Let us study the judgment seat of Christ because believers need to understand it. The Bible says that everything we do will be evaluated, not only what we do, but what we say. Jesus says that at the judgment, every idle word will be evaluated, everything we say. In addition to that, everything we think will be evaluated. Paul wrote, "Therefore judge nothing before the time, until the Lord come, who both will bring to light the hidden things of darkness, and will make manifest the counsels of the hearts: and then shall every man have praise of God" (1 Cor. 4:5). So everything we think and everything we feel will be judged.

What is a good work? What is a bad work? Is a sin a bad work or is a bad work a sin? Anything that falls short of the mark is a sin. So anyone who says our sins will not be brought before us at the judgment seat of Christ doesn't understand what sin is. Any work I do that falls short is sin. If I try to win someone to the Lord and I try to do it for my own glory, in the energy of the flesh, this is sin because it falls short of the mark. That's what the word sin means. It means "to miss the mark," or not to measure up to the standard of Christ. We come short of the glory of God when we do that. Therefore to say that we are never going to see our sins at the judgment seat of Christ is very far from the truth. We certainly will.

The Bible says that if we judge our own sin we won't be judged. Everything I've ever done before I was saved, I'll not see that at the judgment seat. And everything I do after I'm saved that I confessed, judged to be sin, and asked to God to forgive, I'll not see at the judgment seat. I will see those things I have not confessed and judged because they are going to be dealt with there. They will be burned up. I will not have to remember them through eternity. I'm not going to go through eternity with a guilt complex. Praise the Lord! They are going to be burned up.

If you are saved, you will be part of the bride. We will be prepared for our marriage to the Lamb through the judgment of our works. Also, all those things we think are good, but really are not, will be burned up. Everything you do for your own glory will be burned up. Every time you sang a song or preached a sermon for your own glory, it was not good. Every time you went out visiting just to be seen of men was not good. Every time you tried to win a soul so you could say you did it, even though the Spirit used the word and that person was saved, you'll not get any reward. That will be burned up.

The bride will be made ready through this time of purging. Those things you do for God, but in the energy of the flesh, and not in the power of God, are not good. The Bible says every perfect gift comes from above from the Father of lights. You can't do anything good unless God does it through you. If you are doing something because you love God and because you want to glorify God, but you do it in your own ability, it is not any good. How much of what is done in our churches is going to be burned up? There is going to be very little left. Only that which He does in His power through us is going to be left. If the only thing that will stand the test is what He does, and we get rewards for that, then we don't deserve the rewards. That is why those crowns will be cast at the Savior's feet, according to chapters 4 and 5 of *Revelation*.

Once the bride is purged, she will be dressed in robes of righteousness. "And to her was granted that she should be arrayed in fine linen, clean and white: for the fine linen is the righteousness of saints" (Rev. 19:8). Surely this righteousness is the righteousness of Jesus. However, in the original language, the word translated here is plural, denoting righteous acts. We are going to be clothed in those righteous acts Jesus does through us. Isn't that something? Of course, we are going to get into heaven because of the blood of Jesus, but when we come back to the earth with Christ, the bride of Christ will array herself in fine linen, bright and pure, and this fine linen is the righteous acts Jesus has done through us. That is what the original word in the Greek means. All of our righteousness is as filthy rags, the Bible says. How can we have any pure, bright, clean linen to wear, except He does His work through us?

The Marriage Supper of the Lamb

Verse 9 mentions those who are invited to the marriage supper of the Lamb. "And he said unto me, Write, Blessed are they which are called unto the marriage supper of the Lamb. And he said unto me, These are the true sayings of God. And I fell at his feet to worship him. And he said unto me, See thou do it not: I am thy fellow servant, and of thy brethren that have the testimony of Jesus: worship God: for the testimony of Jesus is the spirit of prophecy" (Rev. 19:9-10). Who is going to be invited to the marriage supper of the Lamb? There will be guests there. Who will they be? The bride is going to be the church. The Father is going to be there. The Old Testament saints will be the guests. He talks about those who are invited to the marriage supper of the Lamb, which in John's day happened after the marriage. The Old Testament saints are not part of the bride, but they are in heaven.

This marriage is going to occur at the end of the tribulation in heaven before Christ comes in His glory. The marriage and the feast are two different things, but they are very closely related, just like a marriage and a reception in our day.

The Coming of Christ With the Saints

After the marriage there is going to be a honeymoon on this earth. It is going to be a wonderful honeymoon. Verse 11 begins John's portrayal of the events following the marriage supper of the Lamb. "And I saw heaven opened, and behold a white horse; and he that sat upon him was called Faithful and True, and in righteousness he doth judge and made war" (Rev. 19:11). This is not the coming of Jesus into my heart because He doesn't come into my heart judging and making war. Many say, "Jesus rules in our heart." Yes, but He does not rule in my heart by judging and making war. In righteousness he judges and makes war. He comes on a white horse.

Notice how Jesus is described in the next few verses. "His eyes were as a flame of fire, and on his head were many crowns; and he had a name written, that no man knew, but he himself. And he was clothed with a vesture dipped in blood: and his name is called The Word of God. And the armies which were in heaven followed him upon white horses, clothed in fine linen, white and clean" (Rev. 19:12-14). Who are the armies that are following Him? The believers. The church will be clothed in fine linen, white and pure, and we will come with Him.

He comes with a rod and He is going to rule with a rod of iron. "And out of his mouth goeth a sharp sword, that with it he should smite the nations: and he shall rule them with a rod of iron: and he treadeth the winepress of the fierceness and wrath of Almighty God. And he hath on his vesture and on his thigh a name written, KING OF KINGS, AND LORD OF LORDS" (Rev. 19:15-16). He does not rule with a rod of iron in our hearts today. His rod and staff comfort me, but it's the shepherd's rod. It is not a rod of iron. No shepherd uses a rod of iron. A rod of iron is a weapon, something used to keep people in order. He doesn't do that in us, so this is not how He rules me. The amillennialist says, "Well, Jesus rules us today. The kingdom is within us. And so He rules in my heart." He *does* rule in my heart, praise His name, but this is not what John is talking about here. This is another kind of rule altogether. He rules with a rod of iron.

Let's try to test out our eschatology and our hermeneutics. There is one principle you lay down and three rules used to test the principle. The principle is that you take everything to be literal unless one of three things is true. First, you take everything to be literal unless the context indicates it should be take figuratively. Second, you take everything to be literal unless the rest of the Bible indicates it should be taken figuratively. Third, you take everything to be literal unless the Holy Spirit, using common sense or other knowledge, like history, indicates it should be taken symbolically.

In this passage we have all three of these. For instance, the Bible says here, "And the armies which were in heaven followed him upon white horses, clothed in fine linen, white and clean" (Rev.19:14). What about the fine linen, white and clean? Is that literal or figurative? It could be literal, but is that the point? The point is seen in verse 8. "And to her was granted that she should be arrayed in fine linen, clean and white: for the fine linen is the righteousness of saints" (Rev. 19:8). The point is that we will come back with Him clothed in righteousness. I had rather be clothed in righteousness than in literal fine linen. You can get fine linen dirty and it can tear. We are going to be clothed in righteousness. That's the point the context indicates here.

Notice verse 15: "And out of his mouth goeth a sharp sword, that with it he should smite the nations." So Jesus will come with a sword sticking out of His mouth and He will fight the nations with that sword. Is that literal or figurative? You can be sure it is figurative, but what does the sword represent? The word of God. The second rule comes into play here. The rest of the Bible indicates it should be taken figuratively. The word of God is called a sharp, two-edged sword. What comes out of His mouth? His word. When He comes, He is going to speak, and the word that He speaks is going to destroy. If there ever was a weapon, it is the word that comes out of the mouth of Jesus. He might quote Scripture, but He is going to speak and that's it. He does not have to quote the written word. Any word He speaks is a sword.

Finally, common sense based on history indicates that this passage is figurative. Do you think that we're going to come back on literal white horses, millions of them? Much of *Revelation* is literal, but the white horse carries an idea that, in the days of John, a general who went to war and returned as conqueror came back

119

on a white horse. As far as white horses were available, his men following him would ride white horses. The signal to the people as they saw them come was that they had been victorious. Jesus is going to come back victorious, and we are going to be victorious with Him.

The Battle of Armageddon

Beginning with verse 17, we see the battle of Armageddon and the execution of wrath. "And I saw an angel standing in the sun; and he cried with a loud voice, saying to all the fowls that fly in the midst of heaven, Come and gather yourselves together unto the supper of the great God; That ye may eat the flesh of kings, and the flesh of captains, and the flesh of mighty men, and the flesh of horses, and of them that sit on them, and the flesh of all men, both free and bond, both small and great" (Rev. 19:17-18). This is not the marriage supper of the Lamb. This is another supper. These birds that fly in the midst of heaven are vultures, — those that eat flesh.

Verse 19 depicts the armies of Satan gathering to fight against Jesus. "And I saw the beast, and the kings of the earth, and their armies, gathered together to make war against him that sat on the horse, and against his army" (Rev. 19:19). The beast is the antichrist. Remember that the Euphrates will dry up so the kings of the East can come over. The kings of the North and the kings of the South will also be there. With the antichrist, they are going to war against the Lord Jesus. He is the one they hate. He is the one Satan hates. These kings are going to be demon possessed. Demons are gong to lead them to do this. They are going to get to the valley of Megiddo. One would have to be a fool to get caught in the valley of Megiddo. I've been there. I'll tell you, that's no place to get caught, but they are going to be led by demons. There are mountains to the South, East and West - a gigantic box canyon. All the kings that follow the antichrist will be there to fight against the Lord, against Jerusalem, and against the saints.

The battle will be short and decisive. "And the beast was taken, and with him the false prophet that wrought miracles before him, with which he deceived them that had received the mark of the beast, and them that worshiped his image. These both were cast alive into a lake of fire burning with brimstone" (Rev. 19:20). The beast was taken. The beast and the false prophet will be cast immediately into *gehenna*, the lake of fire that forever burns with brimstone.

"And the remnant were slain with the sword of him that sat upon the horse, which sword proceeded out of his mouth: and all the fowls were filled with their flesh" (Rev. 19:21). That is not the remnant of believers. That is the remnant of the armies of the antichrist. The Lord will speak and they will be killed. Every one of them will die. Immediately they will go to Hades, not to *gehenna*, but to Hades. Later they will go into the lake of fire.

Let us study one of the most misinterpreted chapters in the Bible.

Chapter 24
The Judgment of the Gentiles
Matthew 25:31-41

Matthew 25 deals with the judgment of the Gentiles. "When the Son of man shall come in his glory, and all the holy angels with him, then shall he sit upon the throne of his glory, And before him shall be gathered all nations: and he shall separate them one from another, as a shepherd divideth his sheep from the goats: And he shall set the sheep on his right hand, but the goats on the left" (Matt. 25:31-33). When Christ comes in his glory is at the end of the tribulation, at which time he sets up his millennial kingdom. Most of the time, the word *nations* is translated as *gentiles*. Therefore, all the gentiles will be gathered, and He is going to divide them like sheep from goats. He will set the sheep on the right hand, but the goats on the left.

The Son of Man will first address the sheep:

> Then shall the King say unto them on his right hand, Come, ye blessed of my Father, inherit the kingdom prepared for you from the foundation of the world: For I was an hungered, and ye gave me meat (food): I was thirsty, and ye gave me drink: I was a stranger, and ye took me in: Naked, and ye clothed me: I was sick, and ye visited me: I was in prison, and ye came unto me. Then shall the righteous answer him, saying Lord, when saw we thee an hungered, and fed thee? or thirsty, and gave thee drink? When saw we thee a stranger, and took thee in? or naked, and clothed thee? Or when saw we thee sick, or in prison, and came unto thee? And the King shall answer and say unto them, Verily I say unto you, Inasmuch as ye have done it unto one of the least of these my brethren, ye have done it unto me (Matt. 25:34-39).

He is talking to the gentiles who have become His sheep. He says that because you've done this to me, you enter into the kingdom. They said, "When did we do it?" He said, "When you did it unto one of the least of my brethren, you did it unto me." How many groups of people are present? Three groups. Who are they? On the left He has the goats, and on the right He has the sheep. He speaks to the sheep and says, "When you did it unto one of the least of my brethren." The third group is the brethren. When he talks about the brethren, He's talking about the 144,000.

Has there ever been a time when people went to heaven or hell because of how good and nice they were to their neighbor? Many of the children of this world give more money to the United Fund than Christians do. People who are atheists, who don't even believe in God, do many of these things. Those who deny the virgin birth are the very ones who practice the social gospel the most. Some say, "Well, if you do trust the Lord then it is going to be seen in the nice way you treat your neighbor." Is that true? How about those who treat their neighbors really sweet and nice but haven't been saved? Is there ever going to be a time when what you do to some people will definitely determine whether you trusted Christ as Savior? There will be such a time during the tribulation, before the Lord comes in His glory to set up His throne upon the earth.

What the gentiles do with the 144,000 will determine whether they have really trusted Christ as Savior. These gentiles who hear the gospel but reject Christ will turn them in. They'll turn them in to the Gestapo agents of the antichrist. They won't give them drink. They won't visit them in prison. They won't hide them. They won't help them when they're sick. During the tribulation, because of fear of the antichrist, those who receive his mark by bowing down to his image will report those who will not receive his mark and will not worship his image. The gentiles who help the brethren will not bow down to the antichrist, will not worship his image, and will not receive his mark. They will be the gentiles who had never heard the gospel before the rapture and who heard the gospel preached by the 144,000 and who trusted Christ as savior. They are among the saved multitudes of Chapter 7. They will try their best to help the 144,000 when they are in need. That's the meaning of this whole passage here in Matthew 25. It has been one of the most misinterpreted passages in the Bible.

I've heard preachers preach that the way to be saved is to be sweet to your neighbor. If we give a cup of cold water, Jesus says we are not going to lose our reward. We are going to receive a reward for giving a cup of cold water to one of God's children. But that isn't the way to be saved. Many people practice these things who've never been born again. There will come a time when what one does to the 144,000 will be determined by what one has already done with Christ.

This particular judgment will be on earth at the end of the tribulation, just as He sets up His earthly kingdom. The church will have already been taken to heaven. The only judgment we are going to stand before is the judgment seat of Christ in heaven where our works will be evaluated to determine our reward in heaven, not our eternal destination.

There will be more than one judgment. Actually, there are more than three. There is the judgment of the fallen angels. There is the judgment of Israel. There is the judgment of believers' works. One who says there is only one judgment doesn't know the Bible very well.

Only these sheep and the brethren mentioned in Matthew 25 will go into the thousand year reign. Those brethren who are still alive of the 144,000 and the multitudes of gentiles who have trusted Christ will enter the thousand year reign of Christ. The Bible says in verse 46: "And these shall go away into everlasting punishment: but the righteous into life eternal" (Matt. 25:46). Those condemned to everlasting punishment are the gentiles on His left, referred to as goats. "Then shall he say also unto them on the left hand, Depart from me, ye cursed, into everlasting fire, prepared for the devil and his angels" (Matt. 25:41). They go to hell right then. There will be no one to enter the thousand year reign who is unsaved.

What kind of world will exist during the millennium?

Chapter 25
The Millennial Reign of Christ
Revelation 20: 1 - 15

Satan Bound in the Abyss

Chapter 20 deals with the millennial reign of Christ. "And I saw an angel come down from heaven, having the key of the bottomless pit and a great chain in his hand. And he laid hold on the dragon, that old serpent, which is the Devil, and Satan, and bound him a thousand years" (Rev. 20:1-2). The old serpent is the one we read about in the third chapter of Genesis. He's the one that tempted Adam and Eve. He's the one that has been the adversary of God throughout history, trying to get back at God all the time. This angel laid hold on the dragon, the old serpent which is the devil, and bound him one thousand years.

The devil is a real person. One can't bind an influence. One can't bind a principle. He is a person. He is not omnipotent, but he is very, very strong. In fact, he is so strong that Michael would not even rail against him. This angel will be given the authority or power by God to bind him. From this we find that Satan is not omnipresent. Most people realize the devil is not omnipotent. They realize he is not omniscient, meaning he doesn't know everything. But they think he is every place at once. However, he is going to be limited to the bottomless pit, the abyss. He's not every place at once. However, his demons cover the earth. One day he will be limited and put into the lake of fire. God can use any kind of chain He desires to bind Satan.

A well-known Bible teacher says that Satan is bound right now. He writes that because Jesus died, Satan is bound by the blood of Jesus. I guarantee you, he can be bound in relation to my life. By faith I can ask the Lord to bind him on the basis of the blood, but Satan does deceive the gentiles. He is not bound like he will be during the millennium. John says he'll deceive the gentiles no more, until the thousand years are expired. This teacher says he is bound today. If Satan is bound now, he is on a very long leash. Look at how he works in this world. Look at how he works in Africa. Look at how he works in the Middle East. Look at how Satan works in Asia. Look at how he works in America, and you tell me that Satan is bound. I'd hate to see him loosed if he is bound today. He is not bound.

Others say there will come a time when emperor worship will cease and there won't be any emperor worship until a little season in the future. They think that is the binding of Satan. Emperor worship in Rome did stop, but emperor worship still exists in this world. Emperor worship had been practiced in Japan for several centuries until 1945. Worship of tribal chieftains in Africa and other places and the worship of men dominate the Hindu religion in India. Many who were worshiped were rulers, simultaneous kings and heads of religion. There has never been a time when emperor worship has not existed since John wrote this. To say that emperor worship will cease for a season is reaching for straws. The Bible says that these things must be "hereafter," according to Revelation 4:1. Also the first chapter says these are prophecies. This has never come to pass. It will not come to pass until Jesus comes in His glory. When He comes in His glory, He will judge the Gentiles. Then Satan will be bound for one thousand years. Is it exactly a thousand years? If one wants to believe it is about 1,000 years, that is okay. However, it has a beginning and it has an end. No one can get away from that. I believe it is exactly one thousand years.

After the thousand years, Satan will be loosed. "And he laid hold on the dragon, that old serpent, which is the Devil, and Satan, and bound him a thousand years, And cast him into the bottomless pit, and shut him up, and set a seal upon him, that he should deceive the nations no more, till the thousand years should be fulfilled: and after that he must be loosed a little season" (Rev. 20:2-3). I want to emphasize the phrase "loosed a little season." We don't know how long a little season is, but he is going to be loosed for a little season after the one thousand years are accomplished.

Many say that there is no such thing as a thousand year reign of the Lord Jesus Christ. John uses the term "thousand years" five times in these first seven verses. Many say, "Well a thousand years, that's eternity. Jesus comes to set up His kingdom. That kingdom is eternity." There's a problem with this way of thinking. I think it is very obvious to anyone who thinks through it logically. The Bible says that the one thousand year period will come to an end, that it will be finished. Satan will be loosed after the one thousand years. How could it be eternity if it comes to an end? This is a period of time that has a definite beginning and a definite end.

The word *millennium* comes from two Latin words. One is *mille*, which means a "thousand," and the other is *annum*, which means "years." We get the word *annual* from *annun*. When you put *mille* and *annun* together, it means a thousand years. When one uses the word *millennium*, he is talking about the thousand year reign of Christ. There is presently a spiritual kingdom in our midst, but there is kingdom that will to come on earth. That is why we pray, "Thy kingdom come."

The First Resurrection

Verse 4 tells who will reign with Jesus for a thousand years. "And I saw thrones, and they sat upon them, and judgment was given unto them: and I saw the souls of them that were beheaded for the witness of Jesus, and for the word of God, and which had not worshiped the beast, neither his image, neither had received his mark upon their foreheads, or in their hands; and they lived and reigned with Christ a thousand years" (Rev. 20:4). These are going to be raised from the dead. John saw these who were beheaded during the days of the tribulation, because they didn't worship the beast or his image and receive the mark of the beast on their hand or on their forehead. They lived and reigned with Christ for a thousand years.

"But the rest of the dead lived not again until the thousand years were finished. This is the first resurrection" (Rev. 20:5). Who are "the rest of the dead?" The lost. They are all who die before the rapture who are lost, all who die during the tribulation who are lost, and all who die at the battle of Armageddon. The rest of the dead will not live until the thousand years are finished. Everyone who is lost will stay in the grave and will not be raised until after the millennial reign.

According to the last part of verse 5, this is the first resurrection. This is not talking about the rest of the dead who will be raised after a thousand years. The first resurrection is talking about that which happens in verse 4: those who lived and reigned with Christ a thousand years. The people who were saved and later killed during the tribulation are raised after the tribulation. Their resurrection is called the first resurrection. Before the seven years, there is going to be a rapture and resurrection. Now we find the first resurrection is after the seven years. That's right. Everyone who is saved is part of the first resurrection. Jesus is a part of the first resurrection. He was raised 2000 years ago. Jesus is the first fruit of the first resurrection.

In Texas we used to plant cotton. We found that very early some of the bolls would open. Then later on a lot of them would open. Pickers would pick them and think they picked all of them. Then some more would open. There is the first fruit, there is the main harvest, and there are those that come later. We call these the gleanings. So Jesus Christ is the First Fruit. The resurrection is likened to a harvest in the Bible. We will be the main harvest, at the rapture/resurrection, and then after the tribulation will come the gleanings, all part of the first resurrection.

Concerning the first resurrection, notice verse 6. "Blessed and holy is he that hath part in the first resurrection: on such the second death hath no power, but they shall be priests of God and of Christ, and shall reign with him a thousand years" (Rev. 20:6).

The second death has no power over those who are part of the first resurrection. They will be priests of God and of Christ and will reign with Him for a thousand years. We can read many things about this particular kingdom. I think it would be well for us to look at Luke 1:30. There are several statements made here by the angel about Jesus. It is a prophecy about Jesus. "And the angel said unto her, Fear not, Mary: for thou hast found favour with God. And, behold thou shalt conceive in thy womb, and bring forth a son, and shalt call his name JESUS. He shall be great, and shall be called the Son of the Highest: and the LORD God shall give unto him the throne of his father David: And he shall reign over the house of Jacob for ever; and of his kingdom there shall be no end" (Luke 1:30-33). When

Jesus came the first time, He was great and was called the Son of the Highest. Because these prophecies were accomplished literally, we can be sure that the remaining two prophecies in this verse will also be fulfilled literally. God will literally give Him the throne of David, and He will literally reign over the house of Jacob forever. His kingdom will literally have no end! The thousand years will come to an end, but not His reign!

Daniel 7:13 portrays the reign of Christ. "I saw in the night visions, and, behold, one like the Son of man came with the clouds of heaven, and came to the Ancient of days, and they brought him near before him. And there was given him dominion, and glory, and a kingdom, that all people, nations, and languages, should serve him: his dominion is an everlasting dominion, which shall not pass away, and his kingdom that which shall not be destroyed" (Dan.7:13-14). Even though Satan will be loosed a little season, when Jesus begins to rule this dominion will be an everlasting dominion. This is the stone kingdom.

Daniel 2:44 explains the stone kingdom. "And in the days of these kings shall the God of heaven set up a kingdom, which shall never be destroyed: and the kingdom shall not be left to other people, but it shall break in pieces and consume all these kingdoms, and it shall stand for ever. Forasmuch as thou sawest that the stone was cut out of the mountain without hands, and that it brake in pieces the iron, the brass, the clay, the silver, and the gold; the great God hath made known to the king what shall come to pass hereafter: and the dream is certain, and the interpretation thereof sure" (Dan. 2:44-45).

In the dream Nebuchadnezzar saw a stone made without hands cut out of a mountain. It knocked down an image that represented the world kingdoms. Then the stone took over and covered the whole earth. That's the stone kingdom, which is led by Jesus Christ. Was Babylon a literal kingdom? Was Persia literal? Was Greece a literal kingdom? Was Rome a literal kingdom? If those were literal kingdoms, then this will be a literal kingdom. It is not logical to say that those were literal kingdoms, but then assume this one is going to be figurative. This, too, will be a literal kingdom. And it will be a theocracy, a literal theocracy. Jesus Christ will reign.

What kind of reign will He have? It will be a time of peace, according to Micah. "And he shall judge among many people, and rebuke strong nations afar off; and they shall beat their swords into plowshares, and their spears into pruning hooks: nation shall not lift up a sword against nation, neither shall they learn war any more. But they shall sit every man under his vine and under his fig tree; and none shall make them afraid: for the mouth of the LORD of hosts hath spoken it" (Micah 4:3-4). His reign will be a time of peace. Has that ever been accomplished? No!

Everybody is going to have his own place. It will not be a socialistic government. Everyone will have his own fig tree and his own vine. There will be ownership by individuals. The church will not be participating in this on earth. The bride will be with Jesus. Some ask, "Won't we be governing, one of us governing New York and another one of us governing New Orleans?" No! The bride will be married to Jesus. What does a good wife do? Go all over the world governing places? No. What does she do? She stays with her husband. We will be in Zion with Christ. He will be reigning, and we will be reigning with Him. That's what it means to reign with Him. Does a queen reign with her husband? Absolutely.

People who go into the millennium in their mortal bodies will be rulers over different parts of the world because they have been faithful and true. He can trust them. Those are the ones who will have rulership over many things because they were faithful in a few things. The bride will reign with Him in the place of authority. The others who are still in their mortal bodies, as they go into the millennium saved, will have places of leadership.

Millennial Prophecy in the Old Testament

Look at Isaiah 11:6. "The wolf also shall dwell with the lamb, and the leopard shall lie down with the kid; and the calf and the young lion and the fatling together; and a little child shall lead them." This scripture is not prophesying about a little child leading people to Jesus. I've heard people say that. Rather, it means a little child will lead the lions and wolves. Children will not have to be afraid. The earth will go back like it was in Eden before man sinned. There will be few overt criminal actions. That does not mean that man will not be a sinner. Those people, in their mortal bodies, will still have a sinful nature. They will still have children. They will still live on this earth. The animal kingdom and the earth will be changed. The earth will not bring forth thorns and thistles as it once brought forth. The animal kingdom will not be vicious and carnivorous as they are today since the fall of Adam and Eve when the curse came upon this earth. It will be a wonderful time. There will be no war and almost no crime.

There will be prolonged life according to Isaiah 65:20. A person who dies at one hundred years will be considered a child. People will live to be a thousand years old. God's creation will go back to the time when people lived a long time, as it was before the flood. There are two possible reasons. Evidently, there will be an atmospheric change. Scientists say that the atmosphere in which we now live causes us to die earlier because of direct sunlight. Probably, they lived longer before the flood because the firmament was there, and the sun's rays didn't hit them directly. There will also be healing waters coming out of Jerusalem to keep people healthy. They will live to be a thousand years old. However, there will be light, which will be seven times the strength of the present light. Isaiah 30:26 tells us that.

Isaiah 11:1-5 foretells the coming of a righteous Branch who will rule as an offspring of Jesse:

> And there shall come forth a rod out of the stem of Jesse, and a Branch shall grow out of his roots: And the spirit of the LORD shall rest upon him, the spirit of wisdom and understanding, the spirit of counsel and might, the spirit of knowledge

and of the fear of the LORD; And shall make him of quick understanding in the fear of the LORD: and he shall not judge after the sight of his eyes, neither reprove after the hearing of his ears: But with righteousness shall he judge the poor, and reprove with equity for the meek of the earth: and he shall smite the earth with the rod of his mouth, and with the breath of his lips shall he slay the wicked. And righteousness shall be the girdle of his loins, and faithfulness the girdle of his reigns (Isaiah 11:1-5).

The one who will rule comes as an offspring of Jesse, but this is not King David. David had been dead a long time when Isaiah wrote this. This One is supernatural. Not only will He have great wisdom and power, but He will also be able to rule just by speaking.

Isaiah 11:7-9 depicts this thousand year period as a time of peace:

And the cow and the bear shall feed; their young ones shall lie down together; and the lion shall eat straw like the ox. And the sucking child shall play on the hole of the asp, and the weaned child shall put his hand on the cockatrice den. They shall not hurt nor destroy in all my holy mountain: for the earth shall be full of the knowledge of the LORD, as the waters cover the sea (Isaiah 11:6-9).

There will be peace and a change in the nature of animals, as mentioned previously, and all the earth will know about the LORD. His knowledge will be spread completely over all the earth! This has never happened. It will happen during Christ's thousand year reign!

Satan Defeated Forever

Now let's look back at Revelation 20. "And when the thousand years are expired, Satan shall be loosed out of his prison, And shall go out to deceive the nations which are in the four quarters (zones) of the earth, Gog and Magog, to gather them together to battle: the number of whom is as the sand of the sea" (Rev. 20:7-8). Gog is the prince. Magog is his nation or those who will follow him. Some believe the king of the North is Russia. However, it could be Syria, Iraq, or Iran. There will be another Gog and Magog battle before the millennium. That battle will be Russia, Iran, Iraq, and/or Syria. This Gog could be Satan himself. Many conservatives say that Gog is actually Satan himself, and Magog would be those who follow him.

Where is Satan going to get these followers? At the beginning of the millennium, there will not be one lost person. All the lost will be dead. At the end of the thousand years when Satan is released, he will be able to gather together an army to follow him, the number of which will be as the sand of the sea. Where is he going to get them? People who are born in the millennium will need to be saved just like their parents, just like everybody else has to be saved. They will still have a sinful nature. Man has always been a failure. He was a failure in the garden. He was a failure under conscience. He was a failure under the patriarchs. He was a failure under the judges. He was a failure under the kings. He was a failure under the prophets. He has always been a failure. Man might have said, "Well, God needs to be down here upon this earth so that we could see him and talk with him." Jesus came, and man was still a failure. They killed him! "Well, He was just in one place. He needs to be all over," they might say. Since the day of Pentecost, His Spirit has been in literally millions and millions of people, but man still has been a failure. The gates of hell will never prevail against the church, but man will fail in this church age.

The humanists say, "Let man produce a great society." It will only take them seven years to ruin everything. "Ah, it's the devil. That's the reason we are the way we are. That's the reason we have failed. It is because of the devil." All right, bind the devil. Put him in the bottomless pit and he will deceive nobody. Let's just see what man will do without the devil. Well, they will give feigned obedience. They will feign worship. People will have children. Some of them will be saved, and some of them won't. After the first hundred years or so, there will be many lost people upon this earth. They will marry and have children. By the time the thousand years are expired, there will be millions of lost people. Very few people will be dying. After the thousand years are over, Satan will be able to get many millions of people to follow him. You see, man is a failure. Never will man be able to say, "Well, if you hadn't created the devil, we wouldn't have sinned." Man will always have to say, "It wasn't the devil. I was the one."

Satan will be able to convince the lost to follow him, but notice how long this war will last. "And they went up on the breadth of the earth, and compassed the camp of the saints about, and the beloved city: and fire came down from God out of heaven, and devoured them. And the devil that deceived them was cast into the lake of fire and brimstone, where the beast and the false prophet are, and shall be tormented day and night for ever and ever" (Rev. 20:9-10). The camp of the saints will be in the Holy Land. The beloved city is Jerusalem. What happens? It's a bloodless war. Fire will come down out of heaven and devour them. Everyone of them will be burned up.

Satan will be confined to the lake of fire, where he will be tormented forever! Notice, the antichrist and the false prophet (human beings) will still be in the lake of fire, after a thousand years. No one will be burned up in hell, they will be there forever.

Now, let's see where Hades will go.

Chapter 26
The Great White Throne Judgment
Revelation 20:11 - 15

The great white throne judgment is found next in Revelation 20. "And I saw a great white throne, and him that sat on it, from whose face the earth and the heaven fled away; and there was found no place for them" (Rev. 20:11). This is not the same judgment we read about in Matthew 25. There are many judgments. There might be twelve different judgments. There was a judgment in the Garden of Eden when Adam and Eve were cast out. There was a judgment at the flood. There are other judgments in the Old Testament. There was judgment of our sin upon the cross. Also, when we are taken up to be with the Lord in heaven, there is going to be the judgment seat of Christ when our works will be judged. Then, after the tribulation on earth as Jesus sets up His kingdom, there will be the judgment of the Gentiles on this earth.

However, there will be another judgment that will not be in heaven or on earth, but the heavens and the earth will flee from this particular judgment. It will be in space. This is called the great white throne judgment. The only ones who will be at this judgment will be those who are lost. This is the judgment of the lost. Notice the one who will sit on the throne of judgment is Jesus. Of course, the whole trinity will be there, but in the person of Jesus. There is only one God, but here it will be in the person of Jesus. Why? Because the Bible says that judgment will be given to Him. He will judge those who rejected Him. He came first as the Lamb of God, but one day He will return as the Lion of the tribe of Judah. Right now he comes as Savior, but one day as Judge. And judgment will be given to Him, the Bible says. Of course, in Him dwells the fullness of the Godhead, so the whole trinity is in Christ as He judges. The heavens and the earth will flee from the face of the One on the throne, the Lord Jesus Christ. It is going to be a horrible day for the lost. That doesn't mean that His face looks horrible. I would hate to be lost when His eyes look at those who never receive Him as Savior and Lord. The Bible says the earth will flee. This is just before the time when the earth will be destroyed by fire.

The next few verses provide more detail about the great white throne judgment. "And I saw the dead, small and great, stand before God; and the books were opened: and another book was opened, which is the book of life: and the dead were judged out of those things which were written in the books, according to their works" (Rev. 20:12). It never mentions the living, only the dead. Everyone who is saved has already been raised from the dead, so this is just the lost. These are people who have been physically dead, and they are still spiritually dead. They are separated from God. There will be books opened at the judgment, the books of works, the record of works. Also opened at the judgment of the lost is the book of life. These books will be better than the best and fastest computer ever developed.

"And the sea gave up the dead which were in it; and death and hell delivered up the dead which were in them: and they were judged every man according to their works" (Rev. 20:13). Why are they judged according to their works? Many people try to be saved by their works. All the Buddhists and Hindus are trying to be saved by their works. All the people who are lost in Christendom are trying to be saved by their works. People of many different religions are trying to be saved by their works. If I were judged according to my works, I would go to hell. And so would you. Every one of us would. Praise the Lord, I shall never be judged according to my works. I was judged on Jesus when He was crucified. And He received the judgment for my works. Praise the Lord I was saved by the work of the Lord Jesus Christ on the cross. That is the only way anyone can be saved. So if the person is judged according to his works, he will be lost. Not only that, it might be, as some say, people will be judged according to their works in order that some will receive more punishment and others less punishment in hell.

A person in hell will remember all of his opportunities. Read the first chapter of the *Book of Romans* and see why no one (not even a heathen who has never heard the gospel) can claim excuse.

"And the sea gave up the dead which were in it," so the whole earth is going to give up the dead no matter what the condition the body was in at death; whether they've been burned up, blown to bits, eaten by sharks, or in the grave. The sea gave up the dead which were in it. Also "death and hell delivered up the dead which were in them." In other words, the grave and Hades gave up the dead which were in them, "...and they were judged every man according to their works."

The Second Death

Chapter 20 ends with a description of the second death. "And death and hell were cast into the lake of fire. This is the second death" (Rev. 20:14). All the lost who have died will be brought forth, their souls from Hades, in some kind of a resurrected body but not a glorified body like the saved ones, whose bodies will be like the resurrected body of Jesus. They will not be cast back into the grave, they will not be put back into Hades, but they will be put into the lake of fire. "This is the second death even the lake of fire." That means that they are eternally separated from God. "And whosoever was not found written in the book of life was cast into the lake of fire" (Rev. 20:15).

Someone might say, "But, I trusted Jesus!" All right, let's see if you did. Let's look through the book of life and see if your name is there. If your name is not there, you didn't trust Jesus. So if anyone's name was not found written in the book of life, he will be cast into the lake of fire. The Bible teaches that in order to condemn a person, there must be two witnesses. Two witnesses condemn here. The witness of the books of works and the witness of the book of life. Their works condemn them, and the fact they didn't trust Jesus as Savior also condemns them.

Next, let's study about our final estate in heaven!

Chapter 27
The New Jerusalem
Revelation 21:1-27

A New Heaven and a New Earth

Chapter 21 begins to portray our eternal state. "And I saw a new heaven and a new earth: for the first heaven and the first earth were passed away; and there was no more sea" (Rev. 21:1). Notice the old heaven and the old earth have fled away. When did that happen? It will be destroyed by fire (Read II Peter 3:7,10-13): "But the heavens and the earth which are now... are kept in store, reserved unto fire against the day of judgment and perdition of ungodly men... But the day of the Lord will come as a thief in the night, in which the heavens shall pass away with a great noise, and the elements shall melt with fervent heat; the earth also, and the works that are in it, shall be burned up. Seeing, then, that all these things shall be dissolved, what manner of persons ought ye to be in all holy living and godliness, Looking for and hasting unto the coming of the day of God, in which the heavens, being on fire, shall be dissolved, and the elements shall melt with fervent heat? Nevertheless we, according to his promise, look for new heavens, and a new earth, in which dwelleth righteousness."

What about this destruction by fire? Will the earth be completely burned up? Will it be a complete new creation? Will He take this old earth and renovate it miraculously and change it so it is completely new, or will it be made of other molecules? There are three ways suggested: just the outer crust burned, a complete new creation, or the same molecules and same atoms changed miraculously so that the earth is new. When you are raised from the dead, will you receive another body altogether, or will it be the same body changed into a glorified body? What about Jesus when He received His glorified body? Was that another body, or was it the same body changed and made new?

This issue is not a question of whether you are a conservative who believes the word of God. A man can be a conservative and believe any one of these three things. Many commentaries teach that the crust will be changed or that it will be a complete new creation. Some say that it will be the same earth, completely renovated. Scripture seems to indicate that it won't be just the crust. Just like Jesus has a resurrection body that is the same body made new, and our glorified bodies will be the same bodies made new, the new earth will be made of the same molecules and the same atoms. It still will be a tremendous miracle. Maybe the earth will be blown to bits in an atomic explosion, and God will bring it back together. It will be a new earth, not another earth. Jesus didn't receive another body. If He had received another body, the old body would have still been there in the tomb. It was the same body made completely new. Ours also will be the same body made completely new. I'm not going to argue with anybody who believes it will be another earth altogether that is not created yet. I believe, because of scientific law, and II Peter (see above), that it will be the same molecules made completely new. God created every molecule. He created energy. He created everything, and He could do it again. He could create more energy and more molecules. It might be that He will do it that way, but if He does it by using the same elements, it will still be completely new.

Also the word "new" is the translation of the Greek word "KAINOS," which doesn't mean "another," but the same made new!

The New Jerusalem

Next John sees the New Jerusalem coming down from God. "And I John saw the holy city, new Jerusalem, coming down from God out of heaven prepared as a bride adorned for her husband" (Rev. 21:2). Earlier the old Jerusalem was called Sodom, and now it's called holy. Some conservative scholars believe that this is a symbol of the church, the bride. This verse says "as a bride." It doesn't say the bride comes down as a city. That would mean it was the bride looking like a city. But it is a city looking like a bride. Therefore, it must be a city. There are those who say, "This is the residing place of the saved saints of the church age," but we find that there are people from all ages in it. What did the Lord say to Abraham, according to the book of Hebrews? He promised him a city made without hands. And so Abraham is going to be in it.

This New Jerusalem is a city. I don't know if it is square or a sphere. John doesn't tell us. He writes that it is going to have dimensions in four directions. Some people think it is a square, and others think it is round. It comes down out of heaven from God. It is a new kind of city where we will live, but was it there during the millennium? Some people believe it will be and that He takes it away when He destroys the earth and makes a new heaven and a new earth. That's the reason, they say, it comes down out of heaven from God again and hovers over the earth as a satellite. God doesn't tell us everything about this. Many people believe that during the millennium we'll be on this sphere and it will be a satellite right over the Holy Land. We'll be able to go to the earth and back and forth, but those who are in their natural bodies can't do that. I don't know if this is correct or not, but I know this: when the new heaven and the new earth come, it is going to be a new city, the New Jerusalem.

The Beauty of the New City

As we study Revelation 21, read about the beauty of the new city. Beginning with verse 18, he wrote, "And the building of the wall thereof was jasper: and the city was pure gold, like unto pure glass...." The idea of the wall of jasper is in line with the rest of the city, which is clear as crystal. He could see the illumination through it as he was looking on it from the outside. It will be a city that is clear. One can see the light coming through it. The city itself, the Bible says, "was pure gold, like unto pure glass." It was gold that John could see through like glass. It was something he had never seen before. He is trying to describe in earthly language a heavenly scene he experiences. Evidently it was something fantastic: gold in its beauty and yet clear as glass, transparent like glass. There is a constant mention of transparency. The city is designed to transmit the glory of God in the form of this unhindered light as John saw it from a distance. Imagine the illumination of the city, as you see the light and the walls of jasper and the city itself in beautiful gold, but so transparent you can see through it.

Notice the foundation in verse 19. "The foundations of the wall of the city were adorned with all manner of precious stones. The first foundation was jasper; the second, sapphire; the third...," and it describes each of the twelve stones. What does it mean, the idea of twelve? There were twelve of many things in the Bible — tribes, apostles, and so on. However, here John is referring to twelve in apocalyptic literature. Seven emphasizes perfection and twelve emphasizes completion. The foundation was complete.

Many people think it would be tiers, with foundations at the end, one-third of the way down, two-thirds of the way down, and then another at the end of the wall. That is the way many people build houses, but when you build something like a city, it is not done like that. One has to start with the bed rock. These stones are precious stones that were laid layer upon layer. Imagine twelve layers of precious stones with the light from the city playing on those precious stones. I have a diamond my mother gave me, and once in awhile the light will hit it. Suppose it were several tons of diamonds and several tons of ruby and several tons of sapphire. Imagine several tons with the light playing on the jasper walls and the transparent gold and all those beautiful precious foundation stones. What beauty he must have seen!

John is describing it, and I don't know if some of this is symbolic, but I believe it will be a wonderful place, and it will be a literal city. Just try to picture the light of the glory of God in this transparent city playing upon those beautiful precious stones. The idea is that it is completely perfect in its foundation. The foundation is precious. The beautiful reflection of these precious stones relates to God's holiness.

Next, look at the gates to the city. "And the twelve gates were twelve pearls; each one of the several gates was of one pearl: and the street of the city was pure gold, as it were transparent glass" (Rev. 21:21). These gates, we find later, will be open all the time. How is a pearl made? A grain of sand gets inside an oyster shell.

Because this grain of sand is painful to the oyster, a pearl is formed by the secretion of the oyster around the grain of sand. This is God's provision for the suffering of the oyster, so it would be rounded off and smoothed instead of a rough grain of sand. The pearl is the result of the suffering of an oyster.

The idea of suffering also relates to our means of entrance into the city. How do we get into the city? Through the suffering of our Lord Jesus Christ. As a pearl is the result of the suffering and God's provision for the oyster, so our entrance into the city is the direct result of Christ's suffering on the cross, and God's provision for us. The pearl is a symbol of the suffering of Christ. Like the oyster produces the pearl through his suffering, Jesus Christ, who is the gate, provides the way for us to enter into the New Jerusalem through His suffering. Also, remember that twelve represents completion, so it is significant that there are twelve gates to the city.

God's Glory in New Jerusalem

Verse 20 reveals that there is no need for a temple within the city. "And I saw no temple therein." In the millennium there will be a temple, and the Lord Himself will reign from that temple. Yes, there will be a temple during the millennium where people can come and see Jesus and worship Him. That will not be the case in the New Jerusalem. There will be no need for a temple. Notice the first words there in verse 22, "And I saw...." Every time John says "and I saw," there is a new and important detail of divine revelation about to be given. John says, "And I saw no temple therein: for the Lord God the Almighty, and the Lamb, are the temple thereof." There is no need for a mediator in this city.

The word *temple* is a translation of the Greek word that means "dwelling place" or sanctuary. An auditorium is not a sanctuary. In the Old Testament, the Holy of Holies was "The sanctuary," which means dedicated place. There are many denominations that build beautiful buildings, and members call these buildings sanctuaries. They are not sanctuaries at all. Do not call an auditorium a sanctuary. The building was made as a place to hear the word of God, to sing and to worship. It could not be a sanctuary because my body is the sanctuary, the dwelling place of God. One day there will be no need for a sanctuary or dwelling place because, in this New Jerusalem, we will have this most sacred, intimate fellowship with the Lord forever. Since there will be no need for any kind of mediator, there will be no need for a temple.

Notice what John says in relation to the light of the city in verse 23: "And the city hath no need of the sun, neither of the moon, to shine upon it: for the glory of God did lighten it, and the lamp thereof is the Lamb." There will be no need for light. In the first nine verses of John's gospel, he talks about the fact that in Christ (logos) is light. John 1:7-9 says, that John the Baptist "came to bear witness of the light that was the true Light, which lighteth every man that cometh into the world." Jesus Christ, The Son of God, is always the light. He always has been and always will be.

John 3:19 also identifies Jesus as the Light. "And this is the condemnation, that light is come into the world, and men loved darkness rather than light, because their deeds were evil." Jesus is the light. Jesus Himself claims He is the light in John 8:12. "Then spake Jesus again unto them, saying I am the light of the world; he that followeth me shall not walk in darkness, but shall have the light of life." This light of life is Jesus, and He lights every born again believer. Christ will be the one Who lights this whole city. In John 12:35, Jesus again identifies Himself as the Light: "Jesus said unto them, Yet a little while is the light with you. Walk while ye have the light, lest darkness come upon you: for he that walketh in darkness knoweth not whither he goeth." There is another wonderful passage in I John 1:5: "This then is the message which we have heard of him, and declare unto you, that God is light, and in him is no darkness at all." It is more than the physical illumination that we see.

What about the access to the city? Notice verse 25. "And the gates thereof shall in no wise be shut by day." What about the night? "And there shall be no night there." So the gates will never close. There is nothing to keep people out, and there will be a continual day.

During the thousand year reign, there will be a distinction between day and night. Days and nights would have to exist to have a year, to have a thousand years. There will be the sun, the moon, and the stars during the millennial reign. However, in the New Jerusalem, there is no need for the moon and no need for the sun because in the New Jerusalem Jesus Christ, God Himself, will be the light, so there will be no night there. Believe it or not, there will be no need for sleep because we will have our glorified bodies. There will be continual activity because, like the angels, we will have no need to sleep.

John continues, "And they shall bring the glory and honor of the nations into it." The word translated "nations," is the Greek word *ethnos*, which means "gentiles." God has a purpose for the gentiles. They will glorify Him, and they will be able to come into the city. All will come in through the same gates of pearl. These are not gates made out of a thousand pearls. There will be one pearl for every gate, indicating the tremendous suffering of the Lord Jesus Christ. The gentiles will come in.

The Gentiles are not abominable and unclean when the Lord declares them to be righteous. John says, "And there shall in no wise enter into it anything unclean." There will be no evil there. Even though there is no attempt to keep them out because the gates are always open, there will be no evil there. There will be nothing abominable there. John says, "And there shall in no wise enter into it anything unclean, or he that maketh an abomination and a lie." Once we are in our glorified body, we will not tell any more lies. We will be changed. Those who have not been saved will not be there, but those who have been saved will be there. Be sure you are there! Let's find out how we will live forever.

Let's find out how we will live forever.

Chapter 28
The Final Vision
Revelation 22:1-21

The River of Life

Revelation 22 begins with a description of the river of the water of life in heaven. Verse 1 says, "And he showed me a river of water of life, bright as crystal, proceeding out of the throne of God and of the Lamb." In the eternal state of heaven, water of life will come from the throne of God the Father and of Christ. The Bible indicates that in Christ is life. He is called the Water of Life, so out of the Lord Jesus Christ comes a river, the river that gives life.

This is not the same river we find in the millennium, coming out of the sanctuary (Ezekiel 47). That river will be a fresh river, which will heal the other waters of the earth that are so terribly polluted during the tribulation. This river will be coming from the very throne of God, not from the millennial sanctuary. This river symbolizes eternal life and the present believer's experience of the outflow of the Spirit of God. In heaven Jesus will be on the throne in this eternal state. As it is right now, it will be then, that out of the Lord Jesus will come the water of life.

According to verse 2, physical death will be impossible in heaven because, like in the Garden of Eden, there will be a tree of life. The tree of life will bear twelve crops of fruit, yielding fruit every month. In other words, the fruit will always be available. Those in heaven will eat of this tree of life and not die. The idea that the leaves of the tree were for healing means it will be for health, not for correcting illness. The leaves will have health-giving power. There will be no sickness and, of course, no death.

Look at the third verse where John says, "And there shall be no curse any more...." This describes a time after the millennium because the sinner is cursed in the millennium, but there will be no more curse in heaven because the curse of sin is death. Verse 3 continues, "And the throne of God and of the Lamb shall be therein and his servants shall serve him." Those who are saved are the sons and have great privilege, but they will also be serving Him day and night. Since we will not be in our mortal bodies but have glorified bodies, we will be able to serve Him and not ever get tired.

In heaven there will be blessed fellowship. John says, "They shall see His face; and His name shall be on their forehead" (Rev. 22:4). We will see His face. That means we will have immediate access, and therefore we will be able to have unimaginable fellowship with Him. The idea of seeing His face also indicates that we will know Him even as He knows us. That will make it a wonderful fellowship. In our day no one can see His face in a literal sense, but in heaven it will be a perfect fellowship. His name shall be on our foreheads, indicating that we belong to Him.

In verse 5 John says, "And there shall be night no more; and they need no light of lamp, neither light of sun; for the Lord God shall give them light; and they shall reign for ever and ever" (Rev. 22:5). God will be the light in heaven, and there will be no need for any other light. He will reign there forever and ever. He is the light of the world today, meaning He is spiritual light. In heaven, whether this is spiritual or physical light, the New Jerusalem will not need any other light except the light of the Lord Jesus Christ.

John's Final Commission

Verse 6 begins the final message given by our Lord through His angel to John. Notice the angel's message in the sixth verse: "And he said unto me, These words are faithful and true; and the Lord, the God of the spirits of the prophets, sent his angel to show unto his servants the things which must shortly come to pass." The idea of "shortly coming to pass" means it will come to pass suddenly. In fact, in verse 17 Christ says, "And behold, I come quickly." The word translated "shortly," in the sixth verse, and the word translated "quickly," in the seventh verse, come from the same root in the Greek language. The idea that He is going to come quickly or suddenly indicates that the believers should be on the alert. He is talking about the rapture because that is the beginning of everything. When He comes to rapture the church, He will come suddenly.

Then he talks about the blessings for those who keep the saying. In verse 7 Christ says, "And behold, I come quickly. Blessed is he that keepeth the words of the prophecy of this book." Here is another promise of blessing for those who read and know the book of Revelation.

Then John begins to worship before the angel. Notice verse 8: "And I John am he that heard and saw these things. And when I heard and saw, I fell down to worship before the feet of the angel that showed me these things." John's response was rebuked by the angel. The angel said in verse 9, "And he saith unto me, See thou do it not: I am a fellow-servant with thee and with thy brethren the prophets, and with them that keep the words of this book: worship God." The command "worship God" is in the aorist imperative, indicating that it should be translated like this, "In all worship, worship God."

In verses 10 and 11 John is commanded to proclaim the prophecy. "And he saith unto me, Seal not up the words of the prophecy of this book; for the time is at hand." The tense of the Greek language here indicates it should be translated "do not begin to seal the words of this prophecy." It was intended to be revealed and to be proclaimed, not to be sealed up. If the prophecies are rejected, no other message will work, but everything will stay as it is. It will be status quo. He says in verse 11, "He that is unrighteous, let him do unrighteousness still." The idea of the word still is "even more." Therefore, it could be translated, "He that is unrighteous, let him do unrighteousness yet more and he that is filthy, let him be made filthy yet more, and he that is righteous let him do righteousness yet more, and he that is holy let him be made holy yet more." There is no "either-or" in this proposition. No neutrality is possible. The time is coming, and when it comes, change will be impossible. So he is to proclaim the message until it is too late for any change.

Jesus Speaks

In verses 12 and 13, The Lord Jesus Himself gives a message. He says, "Behold, I come quickly; and my reward is with me, to render to each man according as his work is. I am the Alpha and the Omega, the first and the last, the beginning and the end." In verse 12 He speaks in the present tense, which indicates He is saying, "I am coming quickly." The future is impending, it is almost here, and the judgment seat of Christ will come after the rapture. When the Lord comes, those who are taken up to be with Him in the rapture will stand before the judgment seat of Christ. At that time He will give out rewards. Keep in mind that, even though we are saved by grace, as we stand before the judgment seat of Christ, we will receive reward on the basis of what we do after we are saved. Then He says, "I am the Alpha and the Omega," which means the beginning and the end in the Greek language. He says, "...the first and the last, the beginning and the end." He is the one who created, but He will also be in existence at the very end of the age and into eternity.

Jesus then talks about the two classes that need to be recognized. In verses 14 and 15 He says, "Blessed are they that wash their robes, that they may have the right to come to the tree of life, and may enter in by the gates into the city." This is the seventh and last beatitude in Revelation. The authorized version adds, "Do His commandments." However this is not found in the original language. Those who are blessed are those who have washed their robes. People are saved by being washed in the blood, even though it is true that those who have been saved will characteristically do the works and the commands that the Lord wants them to do. That is a characteristic of all believers, but keep in mind that the first command of all is to trust Christ as Savior. Those who have been washed in the blood have certain rights. One right is to have access to the tree of life. They will be able to eat of the tree of life and live forever. Also, they will have access to the city; they will be able to enter by the gates into the city, which is the New Jerusalem. Unbelievers will be excluded.

In verse 15 we read, "Without are the dogs, and the sorcerers, and the fornicators, and the murderers, and idolaters, and everyone that loveth and maketh a lie." This is the third description of the unsaved in this general context. The other two descriptions are in chapter 21, verses 8 and 27. When He says "dogs," he means men of low character. Actually, in the Old Testament days, homosexuals were called "dogs." So this could be a reference to that. This puts sodomites right along with sorcerers, fornicators, murderers, and idolaters. The one who loveth and maketh a lie is right along with those who participate in what mankind considers more serious sin.

Then Christ gives the final testimony concerning Himself in verse 16 saying, "I, Jesus, have sent mine angel to testify unto you these things for the churches." Keep in mind that this is the first time the word *church* is used since chapter 3. This is after the prophecy, when He gives some exhortation about Himself and also about the message of Revelation. He continues to say in verse 16, "I am the root and the offspring of David, the bright and morning star." This has been emphasized in Ezekiel 36 and 37, especially 38:22-25. In the first part of the sixteenth verse He says, "I, Jesus." This really authenticates the whole book of Revelation. Either Revelation is nothing but blasphemous forgery, or it is the most directly inspired authoritative writing ever given. Jesus continues in verse 16, "I, Jesus, have sent mine angel to testify unto you these things for the churches."

A Universal Invitation

An invitation is given in verse 17. "And the Spirit and the bride say, Come. And he that heareth, let him say, Come. And he that is athirst, let him come; he that will, let him take the water of life freely." This indicates that we, the bride, should give an invitation to those who are thirsty and who want the Lord Jesus as Savior. This is a special invitation for those in John's age, and we are living in the same age, the church age. When the church, the bride gives the invitation and the Holy Spirit is also inviting, thirsty souls will come to Christ, the water of life. There is a three-fold invitation: first to the one who hears, second to the one who is thirsty, and third to anyone who will come. Keep in mind that this water is without cost. This wonderful water of life is taken freely, but someday it will be too late, so the person must come now and take of the water of life.

In the next two verses He gives a final warning: "I testify unto every man that heareth the words of the prophecy of this book, If any man shall add unto them, God shall add unto him the plagues which are written this book." This is the solemn witness of Christ about the sacred character of the prophecy and that any tampering with it would bring very serious punishment. Many critics, especially those who participate in higher criticism, are so arrogant that they tamper with all scripture, especially Revelation, to determine what they think is true and what they think is false. They think they are equipped, because of their education, to determine what is inspired and what is not. In verse 19, He says, "And if any man shall take away from the words of the book of this prophecy, God shall take away his part from the tree of life, and out of the holy city, which are written in the book."

Then the final message and final prayer are found in the last two verses of chapter 22. This is the final message: "He who testifieth these things saith, Yea: I come quickly. Amen: come, Lord Jesus." The One who testifies these things is the

Lord Jesus Christ because He is the One who can say, "Yes: I come quickly." The word translated yea is a participle used to enforce an affirmation and should be translated "surely." The idea is "surely I come quickly." Then it is followed by the word *Amen*, which also means "verily" or "surely." Before and after the words, the idea of "surely" is given to emphasize the certainty of His coming. Then John says, "Come, Lord Jesus." For John, the important event is the rapture. Therefore, he is looking for the Bridegroom to come and rescue the bride and take her to heaven. There she will enjoy deliverance from the tribulation, the wonderful kingdom reign during the millennium, and finally the eternal blessing of heaven.

The final benediction is found in the last verse of the book of *Revelation*. John says, "The grace of the Lord Jesus be with all the saints. Amen." More than any other book in the Bible, the book of Revelation presents the most striking contrast between the grace of God demonstrated in the lives and destiny of the saints and the righteous judgment of God upon the wicked. The grace of the Lord Jesus Christ will be "with all the saints. Amen." Now the word *saint* does not mean someone who is voted to be a saint or elevated to be a saint. The word *saint* in the Bible means those who are made holy. This is done by the blood of the Lord Jesus Christ when one trusts Christ and what He has done for us on the cross. Everyone who is a true believer is a saint, so the Lord Jesus Christ does bring grace to all the saints, to all born again believers. There are Old Testament saints, New Testament saints and also Tribulation saints. Anyone "made holy" is a saint!

A Personal Invitation

I hope you are one of the saints. If you are not, you can trust the Lord right now to be your Savior. You might want to close this book, bow your head, and pray to the Lord. Tell Him that you have sinned against Him and that you no longer want to be in rebellion. Confess that you want to turn around, admit your helplessness, and trust Him to save you on the basis of what He did for you on the cross. The risen Savior is able and powerful enough to come into your life, forgive your sin, change your heart, change your whole nature, make you what He wants you to be, and finally take you to heaven. He is able right now to deliver you, to save you and to give you the power to live for Him! Trust him right now. Keep in mind, Christ will be victorious! Be sure you are in Christ.

Yes, I prayed and asked Jesus to save me. I trust Him to be my savior and yeild to Him as my Lord.

Name_____Date_____

If you are already saved, keep in mind that Christ will come suddenly. We need to witness to our loved ones, friends, and strangers. Soon it may be too late. Also, rest in the "blessed hope" that Christ will come for us. Let us be faithful! This Revelation of Christ gives us the story of what will happen _From Now To Eternity!_